A VOICE
AND A DREAM

A VOICE
AND
A DREAM

The Celine Dion Story

Richard Crouse

BALLANTINE BOOKS • NEW YORK

A Ballantine Book
Published by The Ballantine Publishing Group
Copyright © 1998 by Richard Crouse

All rights reserved under International and Pan-American Copyright Conventions. Published in the United States by The Ballantine Publishing Group, a division of Random House, Inc., New York, and simultaneously in Canada by Random House of Canada Limited, Toronto.

Cover photo © Ron Davis/Shooting Star

http://www.randomhouse.com/BB/

Library of Congress Catalog Card Number: 98-92812

ISBN 0-345-42804-8

Manufactured in the United States of America

First Edition: November 1998

10 9 8 7 6 5 4 3 2 1

Contents

Contents

Contents

Acknowledgments

A VERY SPECIAL thank-you to my editor, Cathy Repetti, for thinking of me for this project.

Thanks also to Beverley Slopen for putting me in touch with Ballantine Books.

I would also like to express thanks and sincere appreciation to:

- Stuart McLean for his support and advice;
- Kathleen Scheibling for her invaluable assistance during the creation of this book;
- Carol Keats for providing indispensable reasearch material;
- everyone at Burrelle's Transcripts for their prompt and courteous service;
- Frances Wood and the gang at Southern Accent for their patience and help;
- Chris Heard for his input and encyclopedic knowledge of the *Titanic*;
- Emmanuelle Suau for her help on the French-English translations.

Author's Note

W RITING A BIOGRAPHY of a well-loved star is a daunting and delicate task. I have been aware of Celine Dion for a decade or more, having followed her rise to prominence on Canadian television and radio. To me, living in English-speaking Canada, she was a shadowy figure, ever-present, but only vaguely familiar. For the 6.5 million people in the province to the east of me, however, she was Queen Celine—the grandest star Quebec has ever produced.

Now, through a regimen of hard work and sheer persistence, she belongs to the world, adopted by fans from Australia to the Czech Republic to the United Kingdom.

It has been an engrossing journey—getting to know Ms. Dion through the writing of this book. Although we've never met, I feel as though we have, and I have come to like and admire her. Her story, as presented in this book, is an inspiration. There are many gifted performers, but Celine has qualities that separate her from the rest of the pack—her work ethic and an amazing enthusiasm for life. These virtues shine through in her interviews and her work. In preparing this book, I have done my best to illustrate her remarkable spirit—sculpting into words her indomitable zest for life.

Of course, Celine is, at least in part, the result of all that came before her—her parents, Adhemar and Thérèse, and thirteen siblings—each of whom must be extraordinary in his or her own right. I hope I have done them justice.

A true Aries, Celine is adventurous, ambitious, enthusiastic, and full of energy. A further study of astrology reveals that those born under the first sign of the zodiac also have a tendency to exercise an iron self-control, to discipline the qualities and proclivities of their characters to the advantage, not the detriment, of the society in which they move. Ms. Dion has used her station in life to help others by supporting a range of charities, including the Cystic Fibrosis Foundation and recently the North Korean Famine Relief. With her singing ability she has made millions happy, enriching the life of anyone who has heard her voice.

Even though her taste in clothes these days runs toward Chanel, she has not lost the common touch. The houses, the money, and the adulation notwithstanding, Ms. Dion does not think of herself as a star, but as a simple human being, equal to everyone else. That she has been able to maintain a level head amid the whirlwind of her career fascinated me, forcing me to dig deep and study her background. What I discovered was a woman who has held on to the family values of her traditional French-Canadian upbringing.

I enjoyed getting to know Celine through newspaper articles, television, and, of course, her records. I hope,

through this book, that you will get to know her, and
grasp what drives her.

—Richard Crouse
Toronto 1998

Prologue

IT'S THE 1997 Academy Awards, and Celine Dion is about to make Oscar history. She is nominated in the Best Song category for "Because You Loved Me" from the Robert Redford film *Up Close and Personal*. During the show she will perform the song, backed by the Academy's orchestra. She will be in stellar company. Scheduled to perform the other nominated songs are superstar Madonna (whose performance in *Evita* was snubbed by the Oscars) and pop journeyman Kenny Loggins.

In the audience at the Shrine Auditorium there are "more stars than in the heavens," as an old Academy press release read. This is Hollywood's big night. It is also a special night for Celine, as it is her mother's birthday. The two have always been close, and Celine has rarely missed being with her mother on her birthday. Tonight, however, Mama Dion will have to watch her famous daughter on television along with an estimated one billion other viewers.

Because it is a live show, the unanticipated frequently happens. This night would be no different. Oscar producers had planned to have Natalie Cole sing "I Finally Found Somebody," from the Barbra Streisand movie *The*

Mirror Has Two Faces. Streisand had refused to sing, furious that she had not been nominated in the major categories. At the last minute Cole called in sick, unable to perform. Just hours before show time Celine was asked to step in and sub for the ill Cole. Such a move was notable. No one had ever sung two songs at one Oscar show before.

With little preparation Celine would hand in two exquisite performances, earning the respect of her fans and peers. After the broadcast *Time* labeled the five-octave singer a "global diva." That praise was second only to a note she received from a new fan. Days after the ceremony a bouquet of flowers accompanied with a letter arrived at Celine's home. "You sang my song beautifully," the note read. "Next time let us make one together. . . . You're a wonderful singer." It was signed Barbra Streisand.

To Celine that was the highest accolade she could receive. Streisand had long been Celine's idol, and now they were equals. Not bad for a girl from a small town in rural Quebec, Canada, who once had a vision of being a star.

CHAPTER ONE

◆

The Lucky One

It was in La Tuque, a small village in Quebec, Canada, in the summer of 1944 that Thérèse Tanguay and Adhemar Dion met and fell in love. Both had grown up in Sainte Anne-des-Monts, a farming village in Quebec's Gaspé region. Following Catholic mores, both had come from sizable families. Adhemar was the eldest of five boys and two girls, while Thérèse was the sixth child of nine.

Fate didn't bring them together until harsh economic times forced both families to relocate to the more thriving La Tuque. One night at a community dance the two joined in an improvised music jam. Thérèse began playing "Le Reel de Sainte Anne," a popular Quebec folk song. Adhemar, who had aspirations to be a musician, accompanied her on accordion. The music swelled, and dancers swirled around them, but they hardly noticed. For the eighteen-year-old Thérèse and twenty-two-year-old Adhemar it was love at first sight. They began courting that night, and a scant ten months later they were married in a Catholic ceremony at the local church.

Although the newlyweds' earliest days had the luster of a fairy tale—the whirlwind romance, weekends spent

3

playing music with their close friends and family—the young couple's first years were marred by financial woes. After the birth of their first child, Dénise, in August 1946, Adhemar struggled to keep food on the table. As with many Catholic Quebeckers, the children kept coming, and although each new birth was a joyous event, the pressure to support the family mounted. By the mid-1950s the couple had four children with another on the way. Adhemar had run out of options for work in La Tuque and was forced to leave town to find work. He found a good job in Charlemagne, working in a factory, which offered lots of overtime. Putting in eighteen-hour days, he was able to make ends meet.

The town of Charlemagne is situated just twenty miles east of Montreal. A small town with a population bubbling just under 6,000 souls, it lacks the sophisticated urban feel of its neighboring metropolis. A full 90 percent of the working-class town's inhabitants are of French origin; 95 percent of them natives of Quebec. A Canadian government study reports that 98 percent of the population count French as their only language, while only one percent of the townfolk are bilingual—able to speak both English and French. As in most working-class environments, the men do the heavy work—construction and manual labor; the women toil at clerical and service jobs.

The family lived in a tiny rented apartment, the five kids sharing a room, Adhemar never home, always at the factory. Late at night when he finally returned he was often too tired to spend time with his brood, often falling asleep without eating. Thérèse longed for the

farm life they had known until the move to Charlemagne—the wide-open space, the simple way of life.

The two conceived a plan to save money to buy a
farm. Every day Adhemar saved bus fare by walking to
and from the job at the factory. He was so committed to
the scheme that even Quebec's cruel winters wouldn't
stop him from making the trek on foot. At the end of
each day he would give Thérèse the forty cents he had
saved by not taking a round trip on the bus. She stowed
the coins the old-fashioned way—in a cookie jar.

It took time, but the determined couple saved enough
to make a $400 payment on a small piece of land in
Charlemagne. Now they had to build a house. With no
extra money to hire carpenters, the resourceful couple
decided to do the construction work themselves.

Since Celine has become famous, the story of the
family home's construction has become part of Quebec's
folklore. Adhemar kept up the punishing pace of
eighteen-hour days at the factory, building the house in
his off-hours. Often he slept for only two or three hours
a night, working on the house until four or five A.M., just
hours before he had to go to the factory. It was Thérèse,
however, who set tongues wagging in the small community. By this time she was pregnant with their seventh
child, but that didn't stop her from wielding a hammer,
banging nails in the roof of the partially built house.

"Never once did my mother let her pregnancies get in
the way of her responsibilities or the needs of her
family," Celine says with obvious admiration in her
voice. Through sheer strength of will, and the determination to move their family out of the squalor of the
small rented apartment, Thérèse and Adhemar built the

house from the ground up, even installing the heating system!

The finished home was a busy place. Seven kids, the oldest just nine years old, kept Thérèse busy while Adhemar worked at the factory. Once the kids had been fed and put to bed, she worked at turning the house into a home. Her flair for decorating on a budget soon turned the new home into a comfortable place for family and friends alike. On Friday and Saturday nights the place would ring with music as friends brought over fiddles, drums, and guitars to jam with the tuneful Dion family. Each child was gifted musically, with mellifluous voices that would soar over the din of the acoustic instruments.

Meanwhile the children kept coming. By March 1968, the couple was supporting thirteen offspring—in chronological order, Dénise, Clément, Claudette, Liette, Michel, Louise, Jacques, Daniel, Ghislaine, Linda, Manon, Paul, and Pauline—with another on the way. On March 30, 1968, at 12:30 A.M., just ten days after Thérèse's forty-first birthday, she gave birth to her fourteenth child, a girl she named after a popular song on the Quebec hit parade, "Celine."

The future singing superstar was the largest of Thérèse's children, weighing in at eight pounds, eight ounces at birth. As was only fitting for a little girl who would one day become pop-music royalty, the French-Canadian Genealogical Society reports that Celine is a direct descendant of French Emperor Charlemagne, who ruled from A.D. 768 to 814.

Scholars from the Genealogical Society also claim to have proof that many Quebeckers, including Celine, are descendants of Catherine Baillon. A member of French provincial nobility, Baillon arrived in Quebec City in 1669 as a *fille du roi* (king's woman). These *filles du roi* were women sent to Quebec as spouses for the colonists. Baillon was just one of more than a thousand women who arrived in the French colony between 1665 and 1673. She married Jacques Mirville Deschenes in 1669, a coupling that produced numerous children.

Ballion's lineage goes back twenty-nine generations, all the way to Bernard, once king of Italy, who died in 815. Bernard was the grandson of Charlemagne, the king of the Franks, who was crowned emperor by the pope on Christmas Day in the year 800.

"These kinds of studies bring to the fore the noble side of Quebec society," says the president of the Genealogical Society, Normand Robert.

The young Celine quickly became the darling of the family, doted on by her siblings. Eldest sister Dénise took on a large part of the parenting duty, and to this day still refers to Celine as "my baby."

"While Mom did lunch or things like that, we'd take care of her," says Celine's brother Michel, now acting as her assistant tour director. "I was in a rock-and-roll band, and I'd bring Celine to gigs with me."

Even with the rigors of raising fourteen children, the oldest twenty-two, the youngest an infant, music remained a central part of life in the Dion household. The weekend jam sessions at the Dion house were now a Charlemagne tradition. With the success of these musical evenings in mind Thérèse and Adhemar formed a group with the children to perform at weddings and parties. It was an extension of the weekend jams but brought in extra money to feed and clothe the kids.

Enveloped by such talent, it was natural that Celine would sing almost before she could talk. Her first word was "Dan," a reference to her older brother Daniel, who spent countless hours playing with her. At nine months she spoke her first sentence, *"Maman, je t'aime"* ("Mom, I love you."). After that there was no stopping her. She absorbed the French language very quickly, often able to memorize the entire lyrics to songs at a very young age.

By age four, with the tutoring of her siblings, she was mimicking the singers and dancers she saw at the weekend parties and on television. Her sister Claudette remembers her singing into a spoon or a fork, pretending it was a microphone. Celine's sisters often adorned her in a pretty frock, applied some makeup, and let her perform, using the kitchen table as a stage. The supportive family would gather round, filling the room with rapturous applause after each tune.

The songs Celine sang were mostly Quebec folk melodies, and while her pronunciation of the difficult French words wasn't letter perfect, she had perfect pitch and could hold a tune. A wide smile would cross her face when she sang, and the joy she felt was immediately passed on to anyone who heard her. Her mother says she knew Celine was destined to become a musician from an early age because of her skill at making "people smile and forget their problems."

Celine made her public debut singing at her brother Michel's wedding in 1973. She was just five years old but brought the house down singing three songs, including Roger Whittaker's hit "Mammy Blue." She captured everybody's heart, letting her natural five-octave-range voice fill the church. Her family was in awe of her talent even then. "It was at that point we realized she would become a famous singer," says Claudette. For Celine, the wedding and a subsequent concert at the La Cachette hotel in Joliette confirmed her desire to become a performer.

Life in the Dion house was idyllic for young Celine. Surrounded by her protective siblings, parents, and beloved collection of dolls—fourteen in all, one for each of the Dion kids—it was a happy, safe place. The outside world was a little less kind. When she was just five years old a terrifying accident rocked the Dion home.

Celine was playing on the street in front of her house as her father and brother Clément worked in the yard. Spying a baby carriage across the street, Celine made a beeline for it. She loved playing with babies and wanted to see what was inside the carriage. She crossed the street despite her mother's warnings never to venture into the road alone. On the other side of the street the baby's mother yelled for Celine to stop, but it was too late. Realizing she had broken her promise to her mother never to go in the street, she froze, unsure what to do. Just then a delivery truck backed into the street. The driver, unaware that a little girl was standing in the road, hit her, tossing her in the air. Celine landed with a thud on her head, knocked unconscious.

Michel, who was in the house at the time of the accident, heard the ruckus and ran out to investigate. He knew Celine was out-of-doors, and prayed that nothing had happened to her. His worst fears were confirmed as he saw his youngest sister lying motionless on the road.

He scooped her up in his arms, rushing her to the hospital. Doctors told the family Celine had severely fractured her skull, warning that she might not fully recover. Two long days passed as she lay still in the intensive-care unit. The family held a round-the-clock vigil at the hospital, weeping and praying for her to recover. Claudette later called those days the "most devastating time in our lives."

Perhaps it was the resilient nature of her young body, but Celine recuperated with no physical damage. Other, later traumas were emotional not physical, but no less hurtful. Leaving the confines of the house to enter school, Celine encountered relentless teasing from her classmates. They called her "the vampire" because of her pronounced front teeth. These taunts were very painful to the young girl, who retreated to the comfort of her family rather than make new friends at school.

Thérèse and Adhemar had managed to save some money from the job at the factory and the family band. Surveying their options, they decided Charlemagne needed a nightspot—a restaurant/piano bar with food and music. They opened Le Vieux Baril. Thérèse would head up the kitchen, Adhemar the front of the house. With the help of their kids, they could also supply the musical entertainment. The place was an instantaneous hit, drawing large crowds night after night.

It didn't take much encouragement for Celine to perform at the restaurant. She loved singing in front of people, and the extra money she made in tips was gravy. Her other brothers and sisters took turns waiting on tables and performing, but Celine was clearly the darling of the customers. She sang a mixture of traditional and contemporary songs, with a strong leaning toward the music of Quebec superstar Ginette Reno.

Like Celine, Reno was a native of Quebec. The daughter of a butcher in Montreal's St. Laurent Market, Reno began performing near her father's shop at a young age, billing herself as the "Edith Piaf of Market Street." A large following developed, and soon she was offered a spot on a local radio show. Her juvenile career was cut short when her voice broke, leading to a six-month "retirement." Reno became interested in singing again after hearing Connie Francis's 1961 hit "Where the Boys Are." Studying with vocal coach Professor Roger Larivière, she ultimately found fame on the Parrot record label, releasing a string of hit albums. Under the guidance of her manager, Montreal's René Angelil, Reno tallied hit after hit in her native province.

Celine was a big fan of Reno's and played her records innumerable times. To embellish her act at Le Vieux Baril, she practiced performing in front of a mirror at the family home. Sometimes she worked for up to eight hours a day! The hard work paid off, as soon customers were calling to make reservations at the club, requesting to see the "little girl with the big voice."

Thérèse and Adhemar battled with the morality of letting their youngest daughter, not yet ten years old, hang out in a bar night after night. It was good for business, but was it good for Celine? The answer came from Celine herself. Thérèse recounts that when Celine wasn't allowed to go and sing at the club, she moped around the house and was unhappy. "I had to let her go to the bar and sing or else she would cry," remembers Thérèse.

Under the watchful eye of her siblings and parents, Celine was allowed to perform, and she packed them in. At age ten she was a skilled performer and a local celebrity, even though she rarely made it to the final set of the evening, as she would already be at home in bed.

Working in the club took its toll on Celine's schoolwork, but she wouldn't have had it any other way. The kids at school were often heartless to her, as young kids are wont to be, and the club provided refuge in a place where she was loved and appreciated. Besides, all she wanted to do was sing. Even then she had her eyes focused on the brass ring. "At school I was sleeping and dreaming all the time," she told Lyle Slack in *Chatelaine* magazine. "I didn't learn anything. For me, singing was the real life, not two plus two equals four." When she fell behind in her studies, her ever-helpful siblings would do her homework for her.

At best, Celine was an average student, but not because she wasn't bright. On the contrary, she possesses a keen ability to learn, and is an extremely sharp individual. Her poor marks could be attributed to fatigue and disinterest. While in school, her mind would drift back to the stage at Le Vieux Baril, the sound of applause still ringing in her ears.

The luminous sound and quality of Celine's voice helped her parents tolerate her grades. When she opened her mouth to sing at the bar, something truly magical happened. Her remarkable range and the emotion she injected into every song was unheard of for someone so young. Whether she was singing a toe-tapping folk song or a heavy-hearted ballad, Celine's voice took on a personality that was beyond her years.

Her parents knew she was special and were reminded of that every time they left the house in Charlemagne. At the grocery store strangers would approach Thérèse, spouting about her talented offspring. At the bar Adhemar had to field dozens of phone calls a day regarding Celine. What time would she be on? What songs would she sing that night? Celine was a prodigy, but as simple innkeepers, what were Thérèse and Adhemar to do with their extraordinary daughter?

It was brother Jacques who made the suggestion to write and record an original song for his youngest sister to act as a calling card for booking agents in Montreal. Thérèse and Jacques pooled their musical know-how and wrote a new song, "Ce n'était qu'un rêve" ("It Was Just a Dream"). Thérèse wrote the words, Jacques the melody, strumming on his guitar. Once they had a rough draft, Celine was called on to sing the new lyric. As Thérèse listened, she furiously scribbled changes in her notebook until she was satisfied with the song. It was an inspirational tune, with a swelling chorus and a melodic verse. Perfect for Celine.

Thérèse borrowed a cheap tape recorder from a friend and recorded "It Was Just a Dream" in the family kitchen, with Jacques accompanying Celine on guitar. Everyone was thrilled with the result. With a minimum of rehearsal the twelve-year-old songstress delivered a vocal so full of emotion that it made her sister Claudette cry the first time she heard it.

After a family meeting it was decided to send the tape to Ginette Reno's manager, René Angelil. Thérèse wrapped the demo tape in a red ribbon along with a note that read, "This is a twelve-year-old with a fantastic voice. Please listen to her. We want her to be like Ginette Reno." Getting Angelil's address off the back of an old Ginette Reno album, Thérèse dropped the package in the mail, and in doing so changed her daughter's life forever. Angelil would become Celine's manager, mentor, and eventually her husband.

CHAPTER TWO

◇

René

RENÉ ANGELIL'S SYRIAN father and Quebec-born mother were a typical working-class family in 1940s Quebec. The senior Angelil toiled as a tailor in a factory, putting in long hours, much as Adhemar Dion had done to provide for his family. Like Thérèse, Mrs. Angelil stayed at home, caring for her sons, René and André. During the lean times the boys were encouraged to work hard and better their lot in life. From the time of René's birth on January 16, 1942, his parents had high hopes for him. They encouraged him to break out of the cycle of menial jobs that had characterized his father's career, get an education, and become a lawyer or accountant.

An industrious, hardworking student, René seemed to be headed on the career fast track. He was ambitious, disciplined, patient, and careful—traits typical of a true Capricorn. (One astrological guide adds that Capricorns are "hardworking, shrewd, practical, and responsible . . . capable of persisting for as long as it takes. The wit and flippancy which is characteristic of Capricorns may make some turn to entertainment as a career.")

René worked in a bank and showed a predilection for working with numbers. He decided to study accounting.

15

To further his chances in working in international finance, he became multilingual, teaching himself how to speak English and Arabic as well as his native French. Everything changed, though, when he enrolled at St. Viateur School in Montreal.

Hooking up with two classmates, Pierre Labelle and Jean Beaulne, he formed an after-school singing group called Les Baronets. Conceived as an extracurricular activity, the band soon started taking up more and more of his time. His parents were dismayed when, at age nineteen, he announced that he was leaving school to pursue a career in the entertainment business. Then came the British Invasion. The Beatles and the Dave Clark Five dominated North America's hit parades, and Quebec, despite the language barrier, was no different. Seeing how popular the Brits were becoming in his home province, the canny René retooled his Les Baronets to resemble the groups from England.

Inspired by the fashions of the British Invasion bands he was seeing on *The Ed Sullivan Show*, René let his hair grow and dressed the band in the latest Carnaby Street clothes. Riding on the coattails of the new sound from across the ocean, Les Baronets worked up a repertoire of pseudo–British Invasion melodies, marketing themselves as Quebec's answer to the Beatles. They scored many hits in the province, including "C'est fou, mais c'est tout" ("Hold Me Tight"), "Ça recommence" ("It Won't Be Long"), and "Twiste et chante" ("Christmas Twist").

Success came quickly, but the trappings of fame and the cutthroat music business troubled the sensitive René. Thrown into a whirlwind of glitz and fame, with all the accompanying vices, he almost quit the music biz for the more sedate world of banking. He enjoyed the attention being in a successful group brought him, but was distressed by the music business's predilection for drugs and alcohol. Often, to provide some sense of grounding, he would invite his mother to accompany him while the band was on tour.

It was around this time that René met a man who would become a business partner and mentor. Ben Kaye took Les Baronets under his wing, applying management skills he learned while reading about Elvis Presley's guru Colonel Tom Parker. He gave the group a professional sheen, bringing their act up to international standards. René watched and learned as Kaye engineered their greatest successes, booking them as headliners at the Steel Pier in Atlantic City and the Caribe Hilton in Puerto Rico. From Kaye, René learned valuable lessons that would come in handy when he took over Celine Dion's career.

By the mid-sixties Les Baronets' popularity had reached almost Beatles-like proportions in Quebec. Counting thousands of teenage girls among their fan base, their concerts were guaranteed sellouts. Young fans danced in the aisles, howling their love for the band at every show. In 1966 some of René's young fans were dismayed to learn he had married a beautiful Quebecker named Dényse. The short-lived marriage produced one son, Patrick.

Growing tired of performing, René called it quits with Les Baronets in 1973 to focus on a second career as an artist manager. He quickly picked up several clients, including Ginette Reno and Johnny Farago. By mid-1974 he was married again, this time to Anne, a television personality. Eventually they had two children, Jean-Pierre and Anne-Marie. Displaying the drive he inherited from his parents, René also became a prosperous show-business impresario. Using the musical training he received in Les Baronets, he produced several records for Quebec superstar René Simard, another of Celine's teenage idols.

Displaying the all-or-nothing attitude that has characterized his music-business dealings, René invested almost everything he had saved from his Les Baronets earnings into Reno's career. Thus it was a shock and disappointment when, in November of 1980, she called him and relieved him of his duties as her manager. The news sent him into a depression, causing him to spend "the worst Christmas of my life." That gloom hung in the air until that January morning he received a demo tape wrapped in a red ribbon, postmarked Charlemagne, Quebec.

CHAPTER THREE

$\diamondsuit$

The Little Girl with the Big Voice

R ENÉ CAREFULLY UNWRAPPED the quaint-looking package. Lots of mail like this crossed his desk—tapes from optimistic parents, hoping René could turn their little boy or girl into the next Ginette Reno or René Simard. Most weren't very good, but he tried to listen to every submission anyway, just in case there was a hidden gem waiting to be discovered.

Snapping the homemade demo into his tape deck, he sat back and listened to Celine's young voice fill the room. Immediately his ears pricked up. Despite the minimal production values of the tape, the emotion and range of Celine's voice shone through. This one was a winner, he thought. Now that Reno was off his roster he needed a new protégée, and his instincts told him he was listening to Quebec's next superstar. Hearing that tape "was the shock of my artistic life," he has said.

He listened to the tape several more times before dialing the number on the handwritten card that accompanied the package. Reaching Thérèse, he arranged a meeting at his Montreal office.

It was a blustery January morning when Celine and Thérèse made the twenty-mile (thirty-kilometer) drive to see René. Celine was wearing a pretty new dress, the handiwork of her mother. Racked by nerves at the thought of singing for a professional manager, Celine asked her mother for reassurance.

"Just be yourself," her mother cooed, holding Celine's hand. "Sing the way you sing for the people at the bar. You'll be fine."

René remembers their first meeting as if it were yesterday. "You wouldn't say she was a cute child," he says, referring to her long, pointed incisors, but adds she had incredible brown eyes. He gave her a pen to use as a microphone and instructed her to sing as though she was in front of a crowd of 2,000 people.

Celine took the pen, closed her eyes, and sang "It Was Just a Dream," the song from the demo tape. René recalls getting goose bumps as he listened. Just like the hundreds of people who had flocked to Le Vieux Baril to hear her, he was impressed by the amount of emotion this twelve-year-old girl was able to inject into the song. She sounded years older than her age. René later stated that Celine's voice was "the most beautiful thing I have ever heard."

"While I was singing he started to cry," remarked Celine years later. "I knew then I had done a good job."

One song was all he needed to hear. René signed her on the spot, telling Thérèse he would make her daughter a star within five years. "I have believed in Celine ever since I heard that song ['It Was Just a Dream']," he asserts.

From the very beginning René took total control of Celine's professional life. Breaking in a new act takes a great deal of hard work, and while neither of them lacked ambition or drive, René knew there was a stretch of rough road in front of them.

His first order of business was to arrange financing to kick-start Celine's fledgling career. Ginette Reno's sudden departure from his management company had left his bank account drained, with little in the way of ready cash. Celine's parents had no extra money to invest, so René sought out alternative means of raising money. What he did next shows he truly believed Celine would one day become a huge star. After being turned down for a substantial loan at one bank, he approached another, using the mortgage of his house as collateral against the loan. If Celine didn't capture the hearts and minds of Quebec record buyers, René stood to pay a very heavy price. His wife Anne agreed to the precarious deal after hearing Celine sing. She had as much faith in the young girl as René did.

With a bulging bank account, René starting putting the pieces of Celine's debut in place. Her voice was rich in tone and power but untrained. With proper study, he felt it could be molded into an instrument of unequaled intensity. To this end he hired famous Quebec vocal coach Cécile Jalbert to smooth out the rough edges of the girl's vocal delivery and tutor her on how to sing for recording purposes. Unlike her formal academic schooling, Celine threw herself into vocal lessons, soaking up all of Jalbert's words and instructions. She also kept up a grueling schedule of piano lessons and regular schooling.

Meanwhile René made plans to record Celine. In another audacious move, he decided to release not one, but two records simultaneously—an album of tear-jerking ballads and a Christmas disc. René oversaw every aspect of the first two records, hiring the songwriters, musical arrangers, and musicians. He would produce the records himself. With so much riding on the success of these records, he was leaving nothing to chance.

Using connections he had forged while working with Ginette Reno, he contacted renowned songwriter Eddy Marnay, a prolific French tunesmith who had penned songs for Nana Mouskouri, Edith Piaf, and Michel Legrand. Marnay was hired to pen several new tunes for the two proposed albums; his heavyweight pedigree was bound to attract some attention to the projects. René knew the impact Celine's voice could have on people since that first meeting in January. He remembered wiping a tear from his eye after she was done singing, feeling if she could have that effect on him, a hardened showbiz veteran, she could certainly stir those emotions in record buyers. He gave careful instructions to Marnay to write songs that evoked emotion, that would bring a tear to people's eyes. Marnay relished the chance to write for Celine. After hearing the early demo he described her as having *"la voix du bon Dieu"* (God's voice).

With Marnay at work writing, Ginette Reno's orchestra leader and arranger, Daniel Hetu, was brought on board to lead the band and handle arrangements for the tunes, including Thérèse's "It Was Just a Dream." As René assembled a team of people to produce the first albums, even his wife Anne became involved with Celine's development. As the star of the well-liked French television show *Les Tannants (The Troublemakers)*, she knew a thing or two about performing in public and in front of a camera, a skill Celine would have to master. Anne told Celine a smile is "worth a million dollars." No matter what kind of day you're having, she advised, always smile, because it "will make your fans happy." Celine took this advice to heart, and to this day it is rare to see her in public without a beaming smile, looking lovingly at her fans.

Finally it was time to introduce Celine to Quebec's public. The timing and venue had to be perfect, and in a stunning coup, René arranged for her to perform on Quebec's most popular talk show. On June 19, 1981, Michel Jasmin, a popular television personality, introduced the thirteen-year-old Celine to the television audience. "For the first time," he said, "we would like to present to you a hot new young talent with a magnificent voice, Celine Dion."

The intensive training under Jalbert, René, and Anne had paid off. To use show-business nomenclature, Celine *killed* the audience, wowing them by producing a huge voice from her frail thirteen-year-old frame. As with the Beatles' appearance on *The Ed Sullivan Show*, or Elvis Presley's on *The Steve Allen Show*, Celine's debut on that TV show was one of those moments in show-business history when the audience knows it is seeing something truly special. The career juggernaut Celine still rides today was launched that night. After the show René could not have been more pleased.

CHAPTER FOUR

◇

A Star on the Rise

SEVERAL MONTHS AFTER Celine's triumphant television debut, record buyers were given the opportunity to buy both her debut albums. *La Voix du bon Dieu* and the Christmas album, *Celine chante Noël,* were simultaneously released in the fall of 1981. Celine was barely in her teens, but already her star was on the rise.

Norman Provencher, writing in *The Ottawa Citizen*, summed up the essence of stardom in Quebec. "For all kinds of reasons," he wrote, "Quebec's star-making machine has always been better oiled and more efficient than the entertainment scene in the rest of Canada. The close-knit organization of rabid tabloids and small regional clubs and entertainment halls can, and do, create big (and quite wealthy) fish in the small pond in no time."

Celine and René understood this, and drove themselves relentlessly, keeping up a schedule of photo shoots, in-store record-signing engagements, and promotional television and radio appearances that would have tired even the most seasoned professional. In keeping this sort of agenda, school became a secondary concern, and Celine's grades fell. Alarmed by her plummeting grades, René hired a private tutor to guide her through her studies. Without the presence of other kids her age in school, Celine was pushed further into the adult world of show business.

"Kids today want to go out and go to clubs and have a drink and try to smoke and have boyfriends," she told *Time* magazine in 1994. "Since I wanted to be on stage, I had to go to bed early. You can't have everything. You have to make a choice."

She has described herself as stubborn and hard-headed, and those qualities were very much in evidence during her years as a child star. From a young age she had decided she wanted to be a singer, beloved by all, and worked single-mindedly to achieve that goal. Eschewing the trappings of most teenage girls' lives—going to the prom, playing sports, visiting friends—Celine showed a total devotion to René, repaying his superhuman efforts to make her a star by working as hard as she possibly could. Her homespun charm made her a role model for her young fans. She spent innumerable hours visiting schools, signing autographs for the youngsters, talking about her love of her family, her disapproval of drugs, and her connection with God.

There was only one flaw in Celine's decidedly grown-up persona: her teeth. Like many thirteen-year-old girls, she was concerned with her looks and constantly embarrassed by her long incisors. Her discomfort with her teeth was exacerbated by a newspaper report that referred to them as a "Quebec showbiz joke," saying she was known as the kid with "vampire fangs." Unnerved by the article, and the idea that people were laughing at her behind her back, she began covering her mouth with her hand or microphone while she was onstage. She began to smile less at public appearances.

"It was a big problem then," she says, "with my public, with photographers. I would listen to some comedian making fun of my teeth on television and I used to cry." One Quebec humor magazine even went so far as to dub her "Canine Dion."

"Many fifteen-year-old girls have to fix their teeth," said mother Thérèse at the time, "but for Celine it was a real problem, all these people laughing at her. You know how young girls are."

Over the next several years braces corrected the problem, and ultimately the offending teeth were capped.

The feverish work pace continued. In 1982 Celine traveled to France to record her third album, *Tellement j'ai d'amour pour toi (I Have So Much Love for You)*. Again using the songs of Eddy Marnay, this album was Celine's breakout disc. René had convinced the Pathé-Marconi record label in France that Celine was a special talent, deserving of their full promotional weight. They got behind the young singer, championing her as a child prodigy. The sales tactic worked and Celine won a Disque d'Or award in France.

Her newfound popularity in France had a trickle-down effect in her home province in Canada. The first two albums had been largely ignored by radio, although she was fast gaining a name in concert and through television appearances. When she was awarded the equivalent of a Grammy Award in France, Quebec radio programmers took notice and began playing her songs. "She did what every Quebec singer dreams of," says Jean-Claude Aubin of Trans Canada Records. "She won a Disque d'Or. That's when we succeeded in convincing radio stations here to promote Celine." With her music now on the radio, *Tellement j'ai d'amour pour toi* was able to earn a Canadian gold record for sales exceeding 50,000 copies.

As if that wasn't enough for one year, the jewel in the crown was still to come. Celine was chosen from a field of 2,000 hopefuls to perform at the 1982 Yamaha World Popular Song Festival in Tokyo. René immediately sensed the difference this exposure could make to her career. He persistently lobbied for his young protégée, eventually winning her a coveted spot among the thirty contestants chosen to attend the festival. It was by far her biggest gig to date. She would be singing live in front of an audience of 12,000 and an estimated 115 million television viewers. She rehearsed like never before, perfecting her moves and vocal delivery. On the big night she was honored with two awards. "Tellement j'ai d'amour pour toi" won a gold medal for Best Song, but perhaps more importantly she walked away with a special Best Artist prize, beating out fellow Canadian Bryan Adams.

The Tokyo festival was a milestone in Celine's young career. It strengthened René's belief that Celine was a singer with international appeal, and that she could perform with the best of them in the world forum. Striking while the iron was hot, he stepped up his efforts to promote her not only in Quebec and France, but the rest of the world as well. She began a promotional and concert blitz that took her away from Quebec for long periods.

In 1983, at age sixteen, Celine played a triumphant six straight weeks at Paris's renowned Olympia theater, the site of Edith Piaf's most famous performances. It is the dream of most French-speaking performers to play the Olympia, and here was the little girl from Charlemagne in a string of sold-out shows. To provide a sense of normalcy, Thérèse always chaperoned her on these long road trips, making sure her daughter was grounded and happy.

Even though Celine was constantly working, the support of her family was crucial to her. "I've been telling my friends and my family, 'If you ever see that I'm changing, please, the best gift you can give me is to tell me,'" she said. "I don't want to change. I don't want this business to change me—I'm so happy this way."

Celine relished her newfound star status, keeping up a strenuous pace of recording and performing. In the three-year span between 1982 and 1985 she recorded and released nine albums, earning praise from critics and fans alike. Reviewer Karen B. Faulkner writing in *Record Collector* noted that all of these albums "married her 'voix exceptionnelle' to an engagingly juvenile and wholesome image." These albums are required listening for anyone charting the course of Celine's life and career. Like a family photo album that maps a person's development picture by picture over a number of years, Celine seems a bit more grown-up on each record. There is a noticeable progression in her vocal development with each new release, the audible sound of someone turning from shy teenager to a polished and savvy young adult.

To look after her voice and avoid vocal strain, Celine

kept up a rigorous training schedule, almost like an athlete preparing for a big game. She did thirty-five minutes of opera exercises a day. Cold drinks, alcohol, and cigarettes were strictly forbidden, and she says she didn't laugh very often—it's hard on the vocal cords. If she was having a problem with her voice, her remedy was to lean over a pot of boiling water for two hours, breathing deeply. Before each show she would eat saltine crackers to moisten her throat. She also reported that she always tried to go to bed early because "it's better for my voice." Every morning she would rise early to practice or study videos of her performances.

She was rewarded for her efforts by the French music industry, who had adopted Celine as their *"p'tite Québecoise"* (little Quebecker). She was the sweetheart of the entire province, walking away with a remarkable fifteen Félix awards between 1982 and 1985 for outstanding musical achievements. She was so popular in Quebec that in 1985 she took home five Félix awards, shutting out all the competition, including Corey Hart, who was an international star on the strength of his hit singles like "I Wear My Sunglasses at Night" and "Never Surrender."

While all her professional dreams were coming to fruition, in October 1985 she realized another, more spiritual dream—an audience with the pope. Celine, her mother, René, and two botanists who created a special rose in honor of the papal visit to Montreal in September of 1984 were invited to a special five-minute meeting with Pope John Paul II in Rome. Celine had sung for the pontiff during his Canadian visit earlier in the year. The audience with the pope was front-page news

in Quebec, a largely Catholic province. They reported
that she kissed the papal ring and presented him with a
framed gold record for "La Combe," the song she sang
during a youth rally for the pope during his Canadian
visit.

"It was an experience we'll never forget," René told
reporters after the meeting. "Though it only lasted a few
minutes, we're still having trouble believing it happened
at all."

The intense workload and world travel finally took its
toll on Celine's academic life. At age sixteen she made
the decision to drop out of school and focus her attention on her singing career. School, she reasoned, "was
taking me away from my happiness, from my dreams."
She wanted to be a star, and she had to pay a price to
achieve her dream. The decision was made to quit school
and concentrate on nothing but becoming a star.

CHAPTER FIVE

✧

Parlez-Vous Anglais?

AT AGE EIGHTEEN, after six exhausting years of hard work, Celine Dion was Quebec's biggest star. She had a closet bursting with awards; she had sung for the pope in front of 65,000 people at Montreal's Olympic Stadium; and her concerts always sold out. Her life was moving at an accelerated pace. "The dream started but it was so fast," she said. "Everything was like fast, fast, fast, fast."

Stardom at that level came with a price tag attached. She had given up a normal childhood—no dates, no after-school activities, no girlfriends to gossip with—but Celine had no regrets. "I missed my family and my home," she says of her formative years, spent traveling around the globe singing to adoring fans, "but I don't regret having lost my adolescence."

To repay her parents for their support and hard work in creating her career, she bought them a house in the tony Montreal suburb of Laval. Later she bought them a second home in the Laurentian Mountains. *Ladies' Home Journal* reported she also gave them $150,000, and habitually buys her mother expensive gifts, such as fur coats. In another display of her generous nature, her thirteen brothers and sisters were given $100,000 each. "She doesn't forget who she is," says René. "That's what impresses me the most."

Nineteen eighty-five saw Celine's latest album, *Melanie,* sell 100,000 copies, earning a platinum record in Canada. After a twenty-five-city tour of Quebec, she and René made a decision that rocked the music industry in her home province: René proposed that Celine take a sort of sabbatical, an eighteen-month rest, during which they would retool her image. She was eighteen, a beautiful young woman, but in many circles she was still perceived as a child star. René knew the track record for child stars becoming adult performers was not good, and he was prepared to do what it took to ease Celine's transition into the adult sphere. To break into the world market—especially the United States market—they would have to break free from her "girly" image and transform her into a woman.

Also, she would have to learn to speak English.

Celine realized this was a risky move. Dropping out of the spotlight for a year and a half could slow the momentum of her career, but she trusted René and his judgment and agreed to the plan. "He's the only one that I will listen to without questioning anything," she declared. After a brief vacation she threw herself into the task at hand. The first order of business was to enroll in a three-month crash Berlitz English course. Growing up in Charlemagne, a primarily French-speaking village, she could speak only a few phrases in broken English.

At the Berlitz School she was a good student. Attending classes from nine to five, Monday to Friday, she soaked up the new language, rapidly becoming fluent. During school hours she was not allowed to speak French, and her instructors spoke to her only in English. In her off-hours she practiced English, talking to René for hours, trying to master the nuances of the language. It was an uphill battle at first, and she admitted it didn't go as quickly as she would have liked.

"When people make jokes in English, I laugh because I want to be nice," she confessed in an interview. "But sometimes I don't understand everything, or else I really want to say something but it doesn't come out as well as I want. . . . I have to pretend I am a strong person. But really I am afraid of making a mistake."

Try as she might, there were some subtleties of the language that escaped her. Tensions mounted at one recording session when producer David Foster made a remark that Celine didn't understand. During the making of one of her first English albums, she turned in an inspired vocal performance. Electrified by what he had just heard, Foster, who believes in positive reinforcement for his artists, praised her, using a slang expression she didn't understand.

"That's bitchin'!" he said, meaning to offer an accolade.

Celine, not understanding the dual meaning of the expression, became upset and confused. She thought she had done a good job on the song and couldn't understand why Foster was criticizing her in such a crude way. She voiced her displeasure, and Foster apologized, explaining what the word "bitchin' " really meant.

Even as late as 1996 Celine was still learning and practicing her English. She told Rosie O'Donnell that she tries to learn new words every day. "I'm getting there," she said with a laugh.

With English lessons well under way, next came the makeover. Beauty consultants were hired to cut her waist-length hair, styling the locks into a short, sassy, sexy new look. She began plucking her eyebrows to accentuate her brown eyes. Makeup artists created a new mature look for her face, teaching her how to apply blush, eyeliner, and foundation. As a child star she had not worn makeup, preferring to present herself as simply as possible. "I was like the child of the Quebec people," she explains.

Clothes were the final piece of the puzzle. Gone were the folksy dresses and little-girl smocks. She went on shopping sprees to major cities—New York and Paris—looking for a new, sexy wardrobe. To paraphrase Mae West, Celine was looking for clothes that were "loose enough to prove I'm a lady, but tight enough to show I'm a woman." This was Celine's favorite part of the makeover. "I don't drink or smoke," she joked, "but I shop. It's my sport." With her typical determination, she worked out constantly, toning her body for the more revealing outfits she would have to wear as part of her new image.

After her eighteen-month hiatus Celine referred to the break as a time to "make a change, to become a woman, to make people forget about me a little bit." She hoped that when she came back, people would have forgotten she had once been a little kid with bad teeth.

Presenting Celine's new image, as both grown-up and English speaking, was fraught with many hurdles. The French in Quebec are fiercely protective of their culture and their language, so Celine's linguistic switch had to be treated delicately. In an effort not to alienate her "Francophone" (French-speaking) fans, a carefully orchestrated public-relations plan was put into effect. In interviews she spoke glowingly of her home province.

"First, I have to tell you that I'm proud to be *québecoise*," she said in one such interview. "I'm proud to have grown up with the Quebec people."

Before hitting the boards and returning to live performances, Celine was offered the role of Elisa in a French-Canadian miniseries *Des Fleurs sur la neige*—an offer that intrigued her. She would be playing an abused woman, something miles away from her own personal experience. It would be a stretch, but Celine decided to give it a try, trying out her experience at wringing out the emotion of song lyrics in the challenging new realm of acting.

With her usual gusto she threw herself into the role, turning in a performance of rare intensity. "There was a scene where I had to run because this guy was running after me," she said, explaining the emotions she experienced while filming the television movie. "I felt goose bumps all over my body, and cold, and I cried for real while running because I was really afraid. I really became that person.

"You know, maybe it's bad to talk about this," she continued with a hint of mischief in her voice, "but it's natural and human, and I have to tell you. When I was running—you know when you're so afraid that you pee your pants? Is there a way to say that in English that's not vulgar? Well, anyway, I swear it's true."

* * *

As much as Celine enjoyed her start on TV, acting was an artistic domain that would have to wait. Right now there were other fish to fry.

With clothing designers, makeup artists, and English teachers handling her personal transformation, René set to work on the nuts and bolts of her new recording career. Summoning up all his powers of salesmanship, he courted the major record labels, looking for a deal. Approaching Sony Music (then CBS), he managed to convince a high-level executive to come see Celine perform in Montreal. The executive walked away from the show extremely impressed. He invited René and Celine to his office to discuss the possibility of a deal.

Celine vividly remembers her first visit to Sony in Toronto, Ontario. She saw gold and platinum records on the office walls. The plaque that really caught her eye was one with a diamond in the middle of the disc.

"I asked someone what it was, and they said, 'It's for Michael Jackson because he sold a million albums in Canada,' " she says, picking up the story. "I said to myself, 'Maybe, just maybe, one day . . .' "

A multialbum, $1 million-plus deal was struck with Sony. "I thought the best company would be that of Barbra Streisand, Michael Jackson, Bruce Springsteen, and Julio Iglesias," said René at the time. She was now among the giants of the music industry, and she had to prove her worth.

"At the beginning of my career I was always regarded as a little child," she said. "I sang mostly ballads, which I still love, but my audience was mostly children and very old people. It was always very difficult for me to get my records played on the major pop stations. Which is part of the reason I decided to change my look and my style."

Incognito, the first release for Sony, was a French album that signaled the change. It was vastly different from her previous Francophone records: *Incognito* caught her in a dynamic mood, leaving behind the balladeering of her teenage records and veering into a more adult contemporary sound. She sang with a new confidence, sounding dynamic and self-assured. The album bursts with urgency and punch, leaving no doubt that Celine can deliver both ballads and dance tunes with equal ease.

Sony and Celine's camp were roused by the public reaction to *Incognito*. Single after single climbed the charts and the album flew out of the stores. A sold-out run of forty-two consecutive shows in Montreal proved that Celine's comeback was complete. One Quebec writer noted, "It became clear that Dion had merely picked up where she'd left off—on top." Celine was a true pop Cinderella. After the album went gold in France (500,000 in sales), René felt it was time for Celine to try for a broader audience. It was time to record an album in English.

In 1988, in a move that echoed her previous success at the Tokyo World Song Festival, Celine was approached to perform at the annual Eurovision competition in Dublin, Ireland. Described as "Europe's Olympics of song contests," the Eurovision competition drew in an estimated 600 million TV viewers and had launched the careers of Abba, Nana Mouskouri, Olivia Newton-John, and Julio Iglesias. She would not be representing Quebec, or Canada for that matter. The offer to appear at the prestigious festival had come from two song-writers from Switzerland. According to contest rules, only the author of the song has to be from the country that is being represented; the nationality of the singer does not matter. The writers had penned a tune called "Ne partez pas sans moi" ("Don't Leave Without Me"), which suited Celine's style perfectly.

On the night of the competition in early May, Celine gave an electrifying performance, earning high points from the judges from each of the twenty-one countries involved in the competition. As the field was whittled down and competitor after competitor eliminated, Celine was left pitted against Scott Fitzgerald, the representa-tive from Britain. As the audience waited breathlessly for the jury from Yugoslavia, the last country to announce its points, Celine was a bundle of nerves. Ultimately her years of experience, and impressive five-octave range, won the day, and she walked away with the top prize. She won the contest with 137 points, narrowly beating Britain's 136 points. Denmark came in third with 92 points, and Luxembourg fourth with 90.

When the winner was announced, Celine said, "I started to cry with joy. After I came back onstage and sang again, I was really frightened because a mob of more than five hundred reporters and photographers threw themselves at me."

The next day her face was on the front page of every newspaper in Britain. While most reviews were raves, there was one display of sour grapes. Proving once and for all that the Fleet Street headline writers never miss an opportunity to be outrageous, one story about Ce-line's victory was titled BRITS HISS SWISS MISS.

Minimal bad press aside, in the coming weeks "Don't Leave Without Me" sold 300,000 copies in Europe. The stage was set for Celine's English recording debut.

CHAPTER SIX

◆

The American Dream

FRESH FROM THE Eurovision victory, Celine started work on her first English-language album. Sony spared no expense on the project, sinking one million dollars into the production at a time when most records were made for $100,000 to $150,000. This investment certified that Sony was grooming Celine for international stardom, a fact echoed by label executives. "We regard Celine as an incredible opportunity," said Paul Burger, president of CBS (soon to become Sony), "and we obviously think enough of her to spend whatever it takes to make her a star around the world." To further lend an air of prestige to the project, Sony hired three heavyweight producers to mold Celine's new sound: Andy Goldmark, Christopher Neil, and Canadian David Foster. Between them they had produced hits for the Pointer Sisters, Mike and the Mechanics, Sheena Easton, Barbra Streisand, Neil Diamond, and Chicago. Celine called working with this powerful trio "one of the greatest experiences of my life."

Recording the album, which came to be known us *Unison*, was a happy time for the young singer, even though her command of the English language wasn't complete and she had to learn many of the lyrics phonetically. "You don't know how exciting it was for a little *Québecoise* to record in the same studio as Barbra Streisand," she told one concert audience, who responded with wild cheers. At a press conference Celine shared a secret dream with reporters. "And for *Unison*, I'm almost afraid to say it," she said, "but my big dream would be to be nominated for a Grammy Award."

The good feelings surrounding the production of *Unison* were marred by press reports in Quebec that Celine had sold out by recording an album in English. Paul Burger addressed the accusation at a press conference in Montreal. "Some people have asked us, 'Why is this album in English?' I believe that music is an international language, but there are some kinds of repertoire where it is important to hear the lyrics. Unfortunately, the primary international language is English, and we made the record in English so we would have the chance to work with the best producers in the world."

In public statements Celine was less reserved than Burger about the language issue. "When I began singing, I was only five years old—that's all I know, singing," she said passionately. "My dream was always to have a career as a singer. That has happened in Quebec, and I love to sing in French. But this new step is very important."

Very important indeed. Everyone in the Dion camp considered this to be the make-or-break album for Celine in English-speaking Canada and the United States. An extensive and expensive promotional schedule was drawn up. For the record's launch, press and radio personalities were flown in from across North America to a ski resort in the Laurentians for interviews, after which Celine was sent on a cross-continent promo blitz. Burger admitted that because of the amount of money CBS had riding on Celine, it considered *Unison* to be a "critical project."

Celine, then twenty-two years old, took all the hype in stride. Years of training in the French market had left her a seasoned veteran, able to handle a press interview with aplomb. "I don't think money when I sing," she said. "For me, the money is not important. I am not a business person. I am a singer.

"I want to be—I have to be—known," she explained. "That's why I'm doing my first English album."

She was reflective about the task ahead and determined to make it. "I have the team, a family, a great manager," she said. "I have songs, writers, producers. I'm young. Without boasting, I think I have the talent. And I'm ready to work very hard."

One interview showed Celine's raw ambition in a humorous way. The interview had been arranged in a busy downtown Toronto restaurant. As Celine and the writer began their lunch, she mentioned that if they were in Quebec, she would be hounded by autograph seekers as she ate. "Here it's more fun for me," she said. "It's a chance to be a little more . . . incognito." Just as she seemed to be relishing the anonymity, and enjoying her ham-and-cheese sandwich, she added, "Of course, I hope that one day they're not going to let me finish my lunch here either." Those days weren't far off, but right now Celine was just another struggling singer, trying to break into the greater North American big time.

In Quebec it was a different story. *Unison* was greeted with favorable reviews and a public willing to buy Celine's records, no matter what language the lyrics were in. Proving that Celine's voice could cut across cultural boundaries, one French critic raved about the English record: "She has at the bottom of her throat an instrument for which the finest performers would foam at the mouth in envy."

By the time *Unison* hit the stores, René was seeking new and profitable ways of investing Celine's money. Given her love of her mother's home cooking, opening a restaurant seemed a natural. René recruited three partners, and the concept of Nickels was born. Company president Paul Sara was brought in because of his decade-long involvement in Montreal's hospitality business. Vice president Peter Mammas, who has worked in restaurants since the age of twelve, was hired to handle restaurant operations and advertising. Lawrence Mammas, who, as the son of a renowned restaurateur, grew up in the business, came on to oversee franchising and construction. Celine and René rounded out the management team, and it is their vision that has driven Nickels from the very beginning.

The five partners developed a theme restaurant, one that looks to the 1950s for inspiration. The first location opened its doors on December 5, 1990, on Côte Vertu Boulevard in the city of St. Laurent, a suburb of Montreal. (In March 1995 the original restaurant was moved to a larger location, expanding from 170 to 232 seats.) Since then the company has grown rapidly, opening forty-five franchise restaurants and serving over six million people annually.

A press release from the company says Nickels incorporates the three major fifties cornerstones: good food, good value, and good times. Design-wise, the restaurants' decorations certainly evoke the spirit of the 1950s—vinyl booths, Cadillacs, Harley-Davidsons, and jukeboxes. Pictures of Marilyn Monroe, James Dean, and Elvis (alongside Celine memorabilia) adorn the walls. The extensive menu features lots of good old-time comfort food with a fifties theme. Customers can order "The Elvis Special," a double burger with melted cheese, coleslaw, and fries. Or maybe "The Brando," a chicken fillet with melted Swiss cheese and mushrooms, is more to your liking. In tribute to their famous shareholder, there is a luscious six-layer chocolate cake on the dessert list called simply "Celine."

Celine has been very active in the company, designing the uniforms for the staff and making personal appearances at different Nickels restaurants.

Thérèse Dion owns and operates one of the Nickels. Celine's sister Linda and niece Brigitte work there. Brother Jacques is a night manager. In all, seven Dion family members are employed by Nickels, making it a family affair.

Nickels has been very successful in Quebec and is now eyeing opportunities outside that province. Future plans involve expanding into Ontario and the United States. A business plan from the company notes, "Nickels has prospered in Quebec with a market of only 6.5 million people. The potential for growth from markets in the United States and Ontario with a combined population of over 260 million people is staggering."

As with all of Celine's ventures, Nickels is a proud supporter of the fight against cystic fibrosis.

* * *

Celine already had a reputation in Canada, but was unknown in the United States. In the competitive U.S. market good reviews are not enough to sell records. They help, but the pop-music landscape is littered with critical successes that have ended up in the delete bins. Remember Steve Forbet? Critics raved over his debut album, calling him "the new Bob Dylan." Record buyers stayed away in droves, and little has been heard from him since. Countless other critics' darlings have learned the hard way that favorable press doesn't necessarily translate into big sales.

The pressure on Celine was tremendous, and that anxiety manifested itself in the form of a dream that she had on six consecutive nights. As reported in *Mac-Lean's*, each night as she was falling asleep she could picture herself perched on the ledge of a high-rise apartment building. Police cruisers and ambulances waited on the street below. A police officer, also on the ledge, would reach out to her, trying to save her life. Instead she would jump. The feeling was so real that she could feel herself falling to the ground, with the wind whipping cruelly against her face. Each night she woke up just before she hit the ground. Obviously, on the inside she was a bundle of nerves about the impending leap into the U.S. market. Outwardly, though, she was the model of composure, and a source of strength for those around her.

Breaking an artist in the United States takes almost military campaign–like precision—a highly trained team of people working for one goal. René understood this, and assembled the best people available to promote

Celine. Because she was already a seasoned pro after eight years of working in Canada and France, she had the experience to wow American television and radio programmers.

To ensure that Celine would have every advantage in cracking the United States market, a large U.S. public-relations company, Rogers and Cowan, was hired to book high-profile promotional gigs for the young singer. The firm is the top of the line in public relations, representing such heavy hitters as the Rolling Stones and Julio Iglesias. It was a costly move but paid dividends almost immediately. On the strength of her single "Where Does My Heart Beat Now?" Rogers and Cowan got Celine booked on *The Tonight Show*.

This was an important step. *The Tonight Show* was the premier television showcase for new artists. During the Johnny Carson years the show was so popular it accounted for a full 15 to 20 percent of the profits recorded for the entire NBC network. It was a prestige show and the perfect venue for Celine to make her American television debut. Several years earlier another Quebec performer, impressionist André-Philippe Gagnon, used the show as a springboard to international fame. Now it was Celine's turn.

Expectations in the Dion camp were high. This was Celine's first exposure in the United States, and the pressure to perform well was enormous. A flop on this show could set her career back to ground zero. Everything had to be perfect. At the Friday-night taping Celine was dressed for success. Wearing a short black ensemble, she waited backstage for guest host Jay Leno to introduce her. Three guests preceded her: rock star Phil

Collins, actor Jimmy Smits, and television veteran Audrey Meadows. Finally it was Celine's turn. After a brief introduction, in which Leno called her "a huge star up there in Canada," Celine strode to center stage and belted out a winning version of "Where Does My Heart Beat Now?"

After her performance Leno invited her over to the desk for a chat before the commercial break. This was a sign that all had gone well; lesser acts were banished backstage without such a visit. Celine looked nervous and enthusiastic as she spoke to Leno. "I'm excited to be on this show," she said as they went to commercial.

The show had been a victory. Producer Fred de Cordova was so knocked out by her performance that he invited her back a month later. The twenty-two-year-old singer had come one step closer to her dream of being a worldwide star. "I want to be a star by age thirty," she once said, and now it looked like she was on her way. America seemed ready to embrace this *québecoise* girl as one of their own.

Back home, though, trouble was brewing. The annual Félix Award nominations had been announced, and this year, for the first time, Celine was up for the Anglophone (English) Artist of the Year. She had already won fifteen Félix trophies for her French records, awards she was honored to receive. This year was different. The nomination for Anglophone Artist of the Year implied that she had abandoned her French audience for the larger English-speaking world.

The selections had been announced weeks before the ceremony was scheduled to take place. Celine and René, so busy with their efforts to launch Celine in the United States, claimed they had not heard of the nomination until it was too late to pull out of the show. "We learned that Celine was an Anglophone finalist while we were aboard a plane," said René in a prepared statement to the press. "It was too late then." That explanation didn't wash with the Félix organizers, who claimed that René had supplied a photograph for the souvenir program weeks before.

In the days leading up to the awards presentation, the Quebec press viciously attacked Celine for running in an English category. One paper went so far as to wonder "whether Celine would cry in English if she won." With the bad press mounting, René felt that she had no choice but to respond to the critics at the awards gala.

The night of the show Celine's voice was hoarse and raspy from a bout of laryngitis. Predictably, she won the trophy for Anglophone Artist of the Year. She surprised the three-hundred-member black-tie audience with her speech. "I cannot accept this award," she said, straining to be heard. "I think my fans understand that I am not an Anglophone artist. . . . Everywhere I go, I say I'm proud to be *québecoise*."

Refusing the award placated the French press, but didn't please the Félix organizers. The association accused Celine and René of "taking advantage of ADISQ [the governing body of the Félix Awards], rather than taking part in it. Unfortunately they deprived in this way all the other winners of the media attention that winning the Félix usually means—attention from which Dion herself has greatly benefitted from in past years. . . . By refusing the trophy, Dion has refused the encouragement of those who have witnessed her career from its beginnings, and who have always supported it."

René countered that he didn't react to the insulting nomination right away "because I said to myself: 'I won't give them the satisfaction of not showing them to be crazy. . . . Either they're all idiots on the committee, and they didn't realize the wrong they did Celine in placing her in the category of Anglophone artist, or they're intelligent and they did it on purpose.' "

The battle of words with the Félix organizers led to the creation of a new category for Quebec artists who sing in a language other than French. Soon the Quebec press labeled the new category "the Celine Dion Award."

With the Félix debacle behind them, a more serious threat to Celine's career was in the offing. The laryngitis that plagued her through the awards ceremony lingered, requiring a doctor's attention. An appointment was made with Gwen Korovin, a New York throat specialist who has treated Frank Sinatra, Luciano Pavarotti, and Cher. To battle Celine's sore throat Korovin prescribed anti-inflammatories and a complete vocal rest. For two weeks Celine sat on a beach in Aruba and didn't utter a single word. She communicated to family and friends through sign language and written notes.

During this time off she developed a code to talk to her mother on the phone. Her mother would ask her questions, and Celine would tap once on the phone for "no," twice for "yes." They were able to have entire conversations this way, and because Celine rarely speaks on the day of a concert, it is a system they use to this day.

Korovin's treatment was effective, earning Celine's

gratitude for saving her voice without surgery. In 1996, when sales of *Falling into You* were skyrocketing, Celine thanked the doctor with a photograph inscribed, "Presented to Gwen Korovin in recognition of your outstanding contribution—50 million albums—December 1996."

Buoyed by the strong showing on *The Tonight Show* and a massive publicity tour, sales of *Unison* took off, pushing the single "Where Does My Heart Beat Now?" to number four on the *Billboard* charts in early 1991. While the *Unison* album was making her name in the English-speaking market, Celine went back to the studio, this time returning to her roots, singing in French.

Dion chante Plamondon is a tribute to the work of legendary Quebec songwriter Luc Plamondon, and went a long way toward quashing the reports that Celine had turned her back on her French fans. Plamondon, who can usually be seen sporting a black leather jacket and dark sunglasses, is one of Quebec's most respected and prolific lyricists, having written tunes for a number of international artists including Petula Clark and French superstar Johnny Halliday. His 1978 French rock opera *Starmania* was lauded for its insightful lyrics and beautiful turns of phrase. The songs on *Dion chante Plamondon* reveal the same qualities. "Je danse dans ma tête" ("I Dance in My Head") is a gorgeous song about a person who re-creates her identity through music and fantasy to save herself from the robotism of modern society. "Le Fils de Superman" ("The Son of Superman") is a sad tale of a boy who puts on a Superman suit and, confusing fantasy with reality, jumps out of a fifth-story window, thinking he can fly.

"I do the French albums because it's my blood and it's my origins and it's my roots," Celine explained to a reporter. "It is a must for me to sing in French in my life. Don't forget. I started to sing in French. I have eleven French albums. The English? I started to sing in English because I was interested to travel the world, and because I love singing in English, too."

The Plamondon album shows Celine at the apex of her vocal powers. The material on her first two English albums, *Unison* and *Celine Dion*, leans toward a dependable mix of ballads and funky material but contains lightweight lyrics. Given Celine's limited knowledge of English while she was recording those albums, she was not able to fully explore the emotional depth of the English lyrics. The songs remain powerful by virtue of her incredible voice, but fall short of the emotion she offers up on *Dion chante Plamondon*. This tour de force album proved popular in Celine's established markets, going gold in Quebec and platinum in France.

Steven Spielberg, the legendary movie mastermind behind such hits as *Jaws*, *The Color Purple*, *Jurassic Park*, and *Schindler's List*, became the next beneficiary of Celine's talent. Spielberg's production company, Amblin Entertainment, had recently wrapped up production on a full-length animated film, *An American Tail: Fievel Goes West*. With the artwork completed, Spielberg turned his attention to the scoring of the movie, specifically the closing song. He made a list of possible candidates to sing it, including Whitney Houston, Dolly Parton, Anita Baker, Debbie Gibson, and Cyndi Lauper. A representative from Amblin said they had talked to "every major female singer in America," including Linda Ronstadt, who had sung the title song in the first Fievel feature. They were all dropped after Spielberg saw a video of Celine live in concert and watched her perform on Canada's Juno Awards. "That's the one we want," he said after the Juno broadcast.

"Obviously, Linda was considered for the title song, 'Dreams to Dream,' in this film," said Paul Faberman, vice president of music for Universal Pictures in Los Angeles. "But maybe they just wanted somebody fresh and new. . . . Celine has one of those naturally gifted, beautiful voices and the song has to be done in a sweet, love-song kind of way," he continued. "That's what they were looking for."

This was an unexpected break that overjoyed everyone connected with Celine. "This kind of exposure is fantastic," said Ben Kaye, René's old manager, now part of Celine's team. "It'll get Celine known by the hotshots of Hollywood and it'll give her worldwide recognition when the film is released."

There was just one hitch. The soundtrack album was scheduled to be released on MCA (which was owned by Universal Pictures), Sony's rival. Spielberg used his considerable influence to help sway Sony Music president Tommy Mottola to allow Celine to do the song. In the agreement Mottola was granted some "financial considerations" as well as permission to include "Dreams to Dream" on Celine's next record for Sony.

Ultimately the song was not used in the movie, because "greater minds than myself felt she hadn't arrived yet," in the words of songwriter James Horner. The disappointment of the rejection by Spielberg was softened by other offers from major studios. If nothing else, "Dreams to Dream" opened the gates for more film work. Soon Disney would come calling.

CHAPTER SEVEN

━━━━━◆━━━━━

Celine Gains Momentum

NINETEEN NINETY-TWO SAW work begin on a second English album, one aimed at continuing the momentum started by *Unison*, which was ranked eighty-third among the top one hundred records of 1991. By this time Celine was more comfortable with the English language and was determined to exert more control over the recording of the disc.

"On the second album I said, 'Well, I have the choice to be afraid one more time and not be 100 percent happy, or not be afraid and be part of this album.' [*Celine Dion*] is my album."

In return for investing $1 million into the *Unison* project, Sony had made several artistic demands—which Celine accepted—to ensure the creation of an album they would be able to promote and ultimately sell. The investment had paid off. Celine had followed the rules, and now she wanted more control. "It's okay to say I feel like doing it my own way," she said.

In recording sessions for the *Celine Dion* album she took less direction from the producers, trusting her own instincts instead. This decision brought new life to the songs. She imbued the tunes with vocal acrobatics and nuances, making them resemble the songs she had recorded for the French market. More top-of-the-line help was enlisted for this project, including Prince, who penned "With This Tear" for Celine, and producer Walter Afanasieff, known for his work with Whitney Houston and Michael Bolton.

In Canada, Celine and Bryan Adams found themselves the subjects of a media tempest in a teapot. Both are Canadian-born performers who base their operations outside of Canada. And in the cases of both their albums, the Canadian Radio and Television Commission denied Can Con (Canadian Content) status. All fifteen cuts of Adams's *Waking Up the Neighbors* disc and several cuts from *Unison* were deemed non-Canadian because they were either cowritten or produced with British or American partners.

According to Canadian law, radio stations are required to play records that are deemed to be Can Con. The law was passed in 1970 to give Canadian music a chance to be heard in its own country. Many bands and artists have benefited from its passage, including Rush, the Guess Who, and both Adams and Celine. The regulation reads, in part, that "at least 30% of the musical compositions broadcast by a station or network operator between the hours of 6:00 A.M. and 12 midnight shall be by a Canadian and shall be scheduled in a reasonable manner throughout such period."

To qualify as Can Con a record must meet certain standards. The instrumentation or lyrics must be performed principally by a Canadian; the music must be composed by a Canadian; the lyrics must be written by a

Canadian; and the live performance must be recorded wholly in Canada. Any record meeting one or more of these conditions qualifies and has a good shot at being programmed on Canadian radio or television. Failure to qualify can hurt a record's chances of being heard.

Celine was hurt and bewildered by the snub from the CRTC. "I think it is a stupid thing," she said. "I'm a singer . . . and [I] always try to sing the songs I enjoy. I'm not going to say to Walter Afanasieff, 'Sorry, Walter, you can't produce that song because it's not going to be Canadian content.' And I'm not going to say to [songwriter] Diane Warren, 'Sorry, Diane Warren, I cannot sing your song because it's not Canadian content.' Come on, this is stupid."

She stuck by her hard-line stance, using only the best people, regardless of nationality, and threw herself into recording the *Celine Dion* album. Refusing to bow to bureaucratic pressure from the CRTC, she made the best album she could. Celine was growing not only as an artist, but as a person as well.

The biggest change in Celine's life during this wild period between 1989 and 1992 came in the form of René (who had divorced second wife Anne in 1985), her manager, and now, love interest.

The two had been inseparable since Celine was twelve years old, although romance didn't enter their lives until she was twenty-one. The relationship changed gradually, Celine told *People Weekly* in 1994. "The hugs just became better," she cooed, "and his kisses moved across my cheek."

No formal announcement was made. Even though

René and Celine were single, René feared people would frown on this new relationship, painting Celine as a Lolita character and him as a Svengali. René feared that any hint of scandal could undo the years of hard work they had invested in Celine's career, and with a new offer on the table from Sony Records, he advised Celine not to go public with their news. In public it was business as usual, and very few people knew about their love connection.

A testament to Celine's huge popularity in Canada came from two unlikely corporate sources. For years Pepsi had been the most popular soft drink in Quebec; then in 1984 the tide shifted and Coke took major market share. To maintain their hold on the soft-drink market, Coke aired very expensive commercials geared toward the French audience. In 1992 the company launched a series of celebrity-driven ads featuring Elton John, Katerina Witt, and through the magic of computers, the late Jimmy Cagney. The ads aired all over the world, except for Quebec, where a different approach was taken. Dave Sanderson, Coke's vice president of marketing, explained that "the Quebec market these days is focusing inward upon itself. That's why we need to use a different approach."

That tactic involved creating ads that featured family gatherings and hockey players in distinctly *québecois* settings, and, of course, Celine Dion. The strategy was to play up to two *québecois* traits, a love of family and a love of hockey. "I don't know of any other market that places such importance on hockey," said Coke's brand marketing director, Douglas Humfires. "Quebeckers have a real pride in their culture and achievements," he added. Celine was brought on board because of her huge appeal to the people of Quebec.

Realizing that the singer was on the verge of becoming a worldwide star, American Express jumped on the Dion bandwagon. In early 1992 they began a program to reward frequent AmEx card users. The plan was simple. The rewards started when one charged $5,000 on your card, but unlike other cards, which offered such incentives as color TVs and travel points, American Express offered prizes that "money can't buy," in the words of Morris Perlis, head of American Express Canada. Incentives included private screenings of hit movies, a ride in a hot-air balloon, a "cook-along" with a world-famous chef, and for charges of $160,000, entrée to a recording session with Celine. All this attention from large corporations like Coke and AmEx proved that Celine was becoming part of the public consciousness and a major celebrity.

With the popular *Unison* and *Celine chante Plamondon* albums behind her and a new one on the way, Sony realized they had a prolific and moneymaking artist on their hands. Her single "Love Can Move Mountains" topped the R&B charts, only the second white artist to do so in recent years. *Unison* sold half a million copies in Canada alone in the first few months of release. To ensure that she wouldn't be tempted to jump ship and sign with anyone else, Sony renegotiated Celine's contract. Rumored to be in the $10 million range for a further five albums, the contract was the largest ever signed by a Canadian artist. Sony Music president Paul Burger wouldn't confirm the dollar amount of the contract—Sony has a policy never to discuss publicly the size of its contracts with artists—but did say that "the contract is a long-term agreement and, without getting specific, it covers many albums in both English and French. . . . We believe this is the most significant contract ever awarded by a Canadian company to a Canadian artist."

On the heels of the Sony re-signing came more good news. Now that Celine had made inroads in the movie business with *An American Tail: Fievel Goes West*, the Disney Corporation came calling. They asked Celine to consider teaming up with an American singer named Peabo Bryson to sing the theme for their new animated feature *Beauty and the Beast*.

Bryson is a South Carolina native who made his name as a soul singer and producer. His work with Michael Zager's Moon Band produced several hits, including "Reaching for the Sky," "I'm So into You," and "Gimmie Some Time." His greatest successes, however, came when he partnered up with female singers for slow soulful ballads. Hits with Melissa Manchester, Regina Belle, and Natalie Cole established Bryson as a viable commodity on the charts, but it was his duet with Roberta Flack, 1983's "Tonight, I Celebrate My Love," that turned him into a star.

René jumped at the chance to have Celine associated with Disney. The cachet of working with the entertainment giant could only enhance Celine's reputation as a major show-business force. The score for *Beauty and the Beast* was written by Alan Menken and Howard Ashman, heavy hitters for Disney, who would go on to score the mega-hit *Aladdin* before Ashman died of complications from AIDS. In *Beauty and the Beast* they crafted a Broadway musical–style score, complete with swelling ballads, comedic tunes, and at least one surefire hit—the title track.

The Disney deal represented a major turning point in Celine's career. She was now being actively courted by the titans of Hollywood entertainment—the very people who epitomized the American dream that she and René were trying to realize. On a strictly business side, *Beauty and the Beast* offered the chance to reach an international audience. "Any way we can broaden awareness of Celine is an opportunity for us," said John Doelp, an executive at Celine's label, 550 Music. "And the movie business is very good at reaching a very large audience."

The business of soundtrack albums blossomed in the eighties and early nineties. The years between 1987 and 1996 saw the sales of soundtracks quadruple. Record companies realized that the equation of soundtrack albums plus a hit movie could equal millions of dollars in sales. In 1984, Prince's soundtrack from *Purple Rain* spawned five Top 40 hits, moving 13 million copies of the album in the process. *The Bodyguard* soundtrack, anchored by diva Whitney Houston's contributions, is one of the best-selling records of all time, having sold more than 16 million copies. The twenty-year-old *Grease* soundtrack is still a big seller, frequently topping the *Billboard* pop catalog charts. Because American movies have an international audience, playing in countries all over the world, it follows that the soundtrack albums will sell wherever the movies are seen. This can be a huge boost to a fledgling career, an almost unprecedented opportunity to reach an international market. Celine wanted a piece of this action and readily agreed to team up with Bryson for *Beauty and the Beast*.

Producer Walter Afanasieff, hot off of the *Celine Dion* album, was recruited to record the duet. He watched the unfinished movie and, armed with a film clip, entered the studio. He insisted on recording the duet live, with both singers in the studio at the same time. Through the magic of editing and studio wizardry it is possible to record a duet between two people who are never actually in the same room at the same time. The late Frank Sinatra's popular *Duets* album was recorded this way. Sinatra would lay down a vocal track, then send the tape to another studio where the other half of the duet would be recorded. Many of the artists featured on that album never even got the chance to meet Sinatra.

But Afanasieff felt that for this song to work, the singers would have to meet and form a bond. "When you're doing a duet," says Afanasieff, "you create so much spirit together." His hunch was correct, and the chemistry between Celine and Bryson shone through on the "grooves" of the record. They produced a romantic movie theme that capped the animated feature, and left audiences feeling uplifted as they exited the theater. Record buyers responded to the Bryson/Dion combo, pushing "Beauty and the Beast" to the top ten all over the world.

Disney threw their full promotional weight behind the song, waging a campaign with the Academy of Motion Picture Arts and Sciences, hoping for an Oscar nomination. The ploy worked, and "Beauty and the Beast" found itself nominated for Best Original Song in 1992. Once again, as with the Tokyo World Popular Song

Festival almost a decade before, Celine found herself competing against fellow Canadian Bryan Adams, who was nominated for "(Everything I Do) I Do It for You," the theme song from *Robin Hood: Prince of Thieves*.

The night of the Academy Awards—Celine's twenty-fourth birthday—broadcast live from the Dorothy Chandler Pavilion in Los Angeles and watched by almost one-fifth of the human race, was a big night for Celine.

"I'm backstage waiting for my turn," she remembers, "and I say congratulations to Anthony Hopkins as he goes by. Then I go onstage and Barbra Streisand is right there, and then I go backstage because I'm done, and Liza Minnelli is right there passing in front of me." Other highlights of the evening included eating shrimp with Patrick Swayze and meeting Paul Newman in an elevator.

Being a part of such stellar company was a dream come true for Celine, who had always been starstruck. As the hustle and bustle of the live presentation unfolded around her, she was in a daze, and it took some time for her to put her Academy Award experience into perspective. "It's a lot. And I'm only starting to realize it right now," she said several months after the event. "I was too nervous, too high, too afraid to take it in at the time. But now when I go to sleep at night I open my eyes and on my ceiling they're there. And I realize I was with them."

And with them she was. "Beauty and the Beast" took home the Academy Award that night, boosting Celine's international career one more notch. Things were moving at lightning speed both personally and professionally. As if performing on the Academy Awards wasn't enough, that same week was her birthday, the *Celine Dion* album was released, her parents joined her in California for the Oscars, and she appeared on *The Tonight Show*. Her life had the sheen of a fairy tale, and she had won an Academy Award, but that was just the beginning.

CHAPTER EIGHT

———————————◇

Top of the Pops

TV GUIDE MAGAZINE has summed up the Grammy Awards succinctly and accurately. "Glamour! Excitement! The most star-studded musical-variety show of the year!"

The most valued prize in the music industry was born in the back room of the Brown Derby restaurant in Hollywood in 1957. The Hollywood Beautification Committee had approached the heads of the top five record labels to make a list of the recording industry's leading lights for inclusion on a Walk of Stars planned for Hollywood Boulevard. At one of those Brown Derby meetings Decca president Sonny Burke suggested that there should be an academy for recording arts, à la the Academy of Motion Picture Arts and Sciences.

All in attendance agreed it was a good idea. Jay Conkling, former president of Columbia Records and the Record Industry Association of Commerce, was approached to set up the academy. *Variety* reported that Conkling "agreed to serve in a temporary organizational capacity to launch a national organization which would include reps of vocalists, leaders, conductors, art directors, engineers, arrangers, orchestrators, composers, producers, directors and instrumentalists." The original five founders formed the National Academy of Recording Arts and Sciences on May 28, 1957, with the best creative artists in the music business as their members.

An award was designed—a composite of the old gramophones once manufactured by Columbia, Edison, and Victor. A contest was held to come up with a name for the award. The prize would be twenty-five top-selling albums. Mrs. Jay Danna of New Orleans was awarded NARAS's first award—the collection of records—for submitting the name Grammy.

From the first rocky years—at the opening awards ceremony the show's producers ran out of presenters and statuettes—the Grammys came to represent the apex of achievement in music. Winners became the elite of the music industry and a permanent part of the history of American popular music.

Jazz legend Count Basie described what happens after your name is called from the stage: "If your name is called, a lot of things happen in a few seconds," he told *Grammy Pulse*, the membership magazine of the academy. "You're numb, there's an explosion, you're with it, you smile, you think this is the impossible dream come true. For a minute or so you're on a par with all those Oscar winners and those cats who went home with Emmys."

Dionne Warwick, an American singer whose work Celine greatly admires, says the Grammys are the industry's most prestigious award. "Being voted 'the best' by one's peers in this profession is the greatest honor that one can hope to receive. With all the other music awards that have sprung up in recent years, the Grammy

is still *the* award. It was the first and original, and when
you receive one, you know you did it right."

Celine had long dreamed of being part of that glamour
and excitement, the acceptance of her peers, the feeling
that "she did it right." When *Unison* was released, she
told reporters she hoped to get a nod from Grammy, and
now she had not one but two nominations.

Winners at the Grammys are decided by the 6,000
voting members of the NARAS. To qualify as a member
an individual must have contributed creatively to at least
six recordings. The final ballots are tallied by an independent accounting firm.

"I don't think about winning," she said of her Female
Pop Vocalist of the Year nomination, "because the other
artists nominated have sold millions and millions of
records, like k. d. lang, Annie Lennox, Mariah Carey, and
Vanessa Williams. Just being nominated is wonderful."
She may have been exhibiting false modesty, as she, too,
had already sold two million copies of the *Celine Dion*
album and was a fast-rising star in the American market-
place. In addition to the pop-vocalist nomination, "Beauty
and the Beast" was up for Record of the Year and Best
Vocal Performance by a Duo.

The three-and-a-half-hour televised awards show was
the most entertaining in years. The show was a feast of
music, ranging from a gospel and classical Handel's *Mes-
siah*, to rap's Arrested Development, to country's Billy
Ray Cyrus, to a Tony Bennett/Natalie Cole duet, to the
Red Hot Chili Peppers, and the night's biggest winner,
Eric Clapton. Host Gary Shandling was in fine form,
tossing off improvised bons mots. After the acrobatics of
Cirque du Soleil's opening number, Shandling quipped,

"I can't watch them because I try to figure out how they do that and it frustrates me. Same as a porno film."

Later in the show, after Eric Clapton had cleaned up, taking home an armload of awards (he would win six in total), Shandling advised the other nominees: "I'll go out on a limb and say if you're up against Eric Clapton in any other categories, I'd go home now."

One of Celine's idols cracked up the audience with a humorous remark. Pulling sister Janet next to him at the podium, Michael Jackson said he hoped to quash one nasty rumor that had been going around Hollywood. "Me and Janet really are two different people," he said, with a trace of a smile on his lips.

Celine looked fabulous and elegant as she graced the stage to sing with Bryson. She wore a see-through vintage 1970s-style dress purchased at a tony Toronto clothing shop. Celine first saw the dress at a photo shoot for a *TV Guide* cover, and instructed stylist Sandra Marquis to buy it for her. "As soon as she saw it she said, 'I want that dress,'" said Marquis, who purchased it on Celine's behalf for $496 plus tax. "She has a beautiful figure," added Marquis. "She's tall, about five-foot-seven-and-a-half, and really thin."

Celine's name wasn't called in the Female Pop Vocalist category (she lost to k. d. lang), but she didn't leave the ceremony empty-handed. She and Bryson split the Grammy gold for Best Vocal Performance by a Duo or Group, an honor that had previously been bestowed to such songs as "Don't Know Much" by Aaron Neville and Linda Ronstadt and "(I've Had) the Time of My Life" by Bill Medley and Jennifer Warnes. "Beauty and the Beast" and the movie's soundtrack album were honored in categories for best children's album, best movie-TV song, and best instrumental track, the last two wins giving Clapton his only losses for the night.

Composer Alan Menken accepted the award for best instrumental version of "Beauty and the Beast," praising his late partner, Howard Ashman. Menken described Ashman's lyrics as "a song about love, and it's a song that is wise and compassionate . . . it's the wisdom of its message."

"I consider myself still as a new artist," Celine said at the Grammys, "but to be part of a classic [song] at twenty-four years [old] is a wonderful thing. I hope 'Beauty and the Beast' follows my career for the rest of my life."

Backstage she told reporters that she wanted to make special mention of "everyone in Canada who believed in me since day one." She added that she "hopes everyone back home in Quebec and Canada will be very proud."

Celine was just twenty-five years old, and had been associated with René for half her life, the last several years romantically. Their affair was hot gossip in Montreal, the whispering gallery of Quebec, but had not yet been formally announced. In public they were careful to avoid intimate contact, and the Grammy awards appearance was no different. René spoke to Celine on the way to the event, warning her that the eyes of the world were on them, so they would not even be able to hold hands. Celine didn't like this arrangement. She was young and in love, and wanted to announce it to the world, but it would take a near tragedy to bring the news to the fore.

The two had kept their affair under wraps for five long years. René insisted on keeping their romance from the public for a number of reasons. First during the fledgling years of Celine's English career, he feared that if the news became common knowledge, the age difference— he is twenty-seven years older—would be harmful to her image. Second, although his second marriage was over well before he and Celine fell in love, René was convinced the press would paint Celine as a home wrecker, a Lolita, and erroneously report that she broke up his second marriage.

A major health crisis in April 1992 persuaded the couple to go public with their love affair. They were in Los Angeles on the night the Rodney King verdict set off the L.A. riots when René suffered a massive heart attack. Celine rushed him to Mount Sinai Hospital, waiting anxiously in the emergency ward while doctors worked to save his life. The experience of almost losing the man she loved fortified her resolve to declare her love to the world. René recovered through a regimen of drugs and diet to unclog the arteries in his heart. "I was lucky, thank God," he said. "That little incident with my heart was a signal. I have to take time off, relax. I am not twenty-nine anymore." After much discussion with René and her family, Celine decided to follow her heart and announce her love.

"René's the best man for my daughter," said mother Thérèse, lending support to Celine, "so why shouldn't they be a couple. It doesn't matter that he's twenty-seven years older—he's a wonderful man."

* * *

Before the announcement could be made, there was more work to do. René convinced Celine to wait until the press launch for her upcoming album before declaring their love.

As with the other English-language albums, the best talent available was assembled for *The Color of My Love*. Once again David Foster was brought on board to produce. Foster has a special affinity with female singers, particularly with Celine. A classically trained pianist, the Canadian-born producer/songwriter has carved a niche as an A-list producer. His work with Barbra Streisand, Toni Braxton, Chicago, and All-4-One have sold millions of copies, earning (at last count) seven number-one hits on the Hot 100 and six Grammys. Music legend Quincy Jones once called Foster "Canada's most valuable export," in reference to the millions of dollars' worth of records whose production team he has helmed.

A behind-the-scenes worker, Foster is perhaps best known to the general public because of an unfortunate incident involving actor Ben Vereen. While driving home one night along the Pacific Coast Highway in foggy, miserable weather, Foster accidentally hit and injured Vereen, sending him to the hospital. Vereen completely recovered from the mishap, and no charges were filed against Foster, but the accident made headlines around the world.

Foster, with the help of Celine and René, began scouting for songwriters to provide material for the record. One of the benchmarks of Celine's success is the willingness of the world's top songwriters to work with her. Like many other of popular music's greats—Rod Stewart, Elvis Presley, and Joe Cocker—she is an interpreter of other people's music, and as a rule doesn't write her own material. Most of her repertoire comes from songs submitted to her publisher and presented to her for approval.

"I receive about a thousand songs a year," she told *The Globe & Mail*'s Alan Niester. "And I do have a lot of people working with me to listen to all those songs. I just don't look [at] who's been writing the songs, I just play the songs that have been put aside for me, about 50 songs. And if [a song] moves me, I wanna do it."

The all-important song selection for her albums is a time-consuming, detailed process that she and René take very seriously. Celine must feel connected to the tune before she will consider recording it. "I don't want a hit; I want a career," she says. "I don't want to sing a commercial song, I don't want to sell ten million albums and three years from now people don't know who I am. I want to sing the songs I chose because I knew I could bring something to it.

"It's like when you meet somebody for the first time and you feel something right about this person. It's not because he has, or she has, blue eyes or green eyes, or short or long or blond or brown hair. The song just feels right. It either works or it doesn't."

If it works, it can mean big bucks for the writer. Since the songwriters earn a royalty for every record sold, placing a song on a multiplatinum Celine Dion record could make them instant millionaires. For example, a newspaper report stated that Canadian songwriter Dan Hill reaped an estimated $1,400,000 in royalties from his song "Seduces Me," an album track from *Falling into You*.

* * *

Foster supplied the title track for the new album. "The Color of My Love" was a tune he had written for his wedding to his wife, Linda Thompson. "René, my manager, and I were working with David and we wanted to hear the song. He played it for us and every time, really, we were crying," says Celine. "We really loved the song. . . . It's a wonderful, wonderful gift.

"We call it our forever song," she adds, "because it's going to be there forever with me." She certainly throws herself into the song. At the end of *Celine Dion: The Color of My Love*, a special shown on The Disney Channel in the United States, she belts out a breathtaking version of the song. At the end of her performance she turns away from the camera to wipe a tear from her face. "I had trouble holding all the emotion inside of me at that moment," she says.

The next tune chosen for the new album was a cover of an old hit. "The Power of Love" had already been a number-one single in Europe for singer/songwriter Jennifer Rush when Celine recorded it. Rush's version sold over a million copies in 1985, making it the biggest-selling single in Europe by a female artist to that date. Unfortunately, the song's excessive length—it clocked in at five minutes and twenty-four seconds—kept it off most major radio stations in the U.S., killing Rush's chance of scoring a smash hit on this side of the Atlantic. "The Power of Love" reached only number fifty-seven on the all-important *Billboard* Hot 100, the yardstick by which the music industry gauges success.

Rush was living in Düsseldorf, Germany, when she wrote "The Power of Love." The Queens, New York, native was trying in vain to secure a record deal with an American record company when her father, an operatic tenor living in Germany, sent one of her demo tapes to the German branch of CBS Records. Signing with the label, she relocated to Germany to write and record her first album. She wrote "The Power of Love" with her boyfriend Steven, a Harvard graduate, in mind. He was only her second boyfriend, and the two are together to this day! About the European success of the single, Rush says, "There was something in that song that touched a lot of people."

The song had two more kicks at the can before Celine came along. Air Supply covered the tune, also in 1985, reaching number sixty-eight on the *Billboard* charts, while Laura Brannigan took it all the way to number twenty-six in 1987. Celine revived the song after hearing Rush's version on the radio. It gave her goose bumps the first time she heard it, and it seemed like the perfect song for her forthcoming album, *The Color of My Love.*

She says she didn't try to top the original, but did want to lend some new emotion to Rush's song. "For me, 'The Power of Love' has to be treated simply in the beginning," Celine explains, "but by the end it's really powerful, so why not open up the pipes?"

"The Power of Love" became Celine's first number-one hit on the *Billboard* Hot 100. "It's a first in the history of popular music in Quebec," said a front-page story in Montreal's *La Presse.* "All indications are that the record will consecrate, once and for all, the chanteuse Montréalaise with our neighbors to the south."

Rush was philosophical about Celine's success with the song. She told reporters that while Celine did a "beautiful job," she would have liked to have taken the song to number one herself. On a humorous note she adds that her family didn't understand why radio stations were playing Celine's version over her own. She says her boyfriend's family called radio stations in their hometown to complain.

American songwriter Diane Warren (who penned Cher's "If I Could Turn Back Time," among others) said, "A song doesn't go to number one unless kids are buying it. Things are just beginning for Celine." She couldn't have been more right.

After the success of *Beauty and the Beast*, more movie work came Celine's way. *The Color of My Love* contained a lush ballad, "When I Fall in Love," recorded for the film *Sleepless in Seattle*. Relying on the winning formula established by the Disney tune, "When I Fall in Love" was a duet, this time with Clive Griffin. That song did well, earning a Grammy nomination for Best Pop Vocal by a Duo or Group and establishing Celine as the queen of the romantic movie theme.

A third single, "Think Twice," written by Brits Andy Hill and Pete Sinfield, didn't fare well on this side of the ocean, but broke new ground for Celine in the United Kingdom. After a slow start—the song sat on the lower rungs of the British charts for sixteen weeks—"Think Twice" suddenly gained momentum, soaring to the number-one spot, where it spent seven weeks. The record books note that Celine became only the fourth female singer in history to sell over one million copies of a single in the United Kingdom. On the strength of that song, album sales took off, eventually pushing the disc to the number-one spot on the album charts. Both the single and the album simultaneously topped the charts, a rare event, equaled only by the likes of superstars like Elvis Presley and the Beatles. In fact, Celine became the first act since the Beatles in 1965 to top both the album and singles chart for five consecutive weeks.

American critics stood up and took notice of something the Quebec press had known for years—this lady has a voice. "That voice glides effortlessly from deep whispers to dead-on high notes," wrote Charles P. Alexander in *Time* magazine, "a sweet siren that combines force with grace. And it is not just a studio creation. . . ."

David Foster went one step further in his praise. "I truly, truly believe in my heart that Celine is the world's next superstar," he said, and he should know, having worked with Whitney Houston, Natalie Cole, and Barbra Streisand. "Celine is right there. She's in that company."

She was on the threshold of becoming the world's next superstar, but Celine never forgot the people who got her there—her fans. Sitting in the back of a stretch limo after one concert in Montreal, she insisted on rolling down the tinted windows so her fans could see her. "What if they can't see me wave back?" she fretted.

Throughout all of this success Celine maintained close family ties. Her brothers, sisters, and extended family provided the singer with a foundation as her life became increasingly more showbizzy and dreamlike. One niece in particular always had a place in Celine's heart. Karine Ménard, the daughter of sister Liette, was born in 1977 with cystic fibrosis, a disease that attacks the respiratory and digestive systems.

As early as 1984 Celine was using her status as

Quebec's best-known singer to publicize her niece's plight. She paid for and ran public announcements, pleading for donations to help fight cystic fibrosis.

Here's an English translation of one newspaper ad: "Dear Friends, when you hear my songs on the radio, when you see me on television, when the newspapers announce to you that I have gained trophies or that I return from Japan, Germany, France . . . you may think, 'That girl is so lucky!' You are right, I consider myself very lucky to live so many beautiful moments. But what would make me happy, more than all the world, would be the discovery, one day, of a remedy for the evil pain my niece Karine suffers from cystic fibrosis. Karine does all she can to fight this disease. I want to help her, but I cannot do everything. I need you, your generosity. Research is our only hope. Thank you with all my heart. Celine Dion."

Aunt Celine did everything she could to make Karine happy. Whenever she was in Montreal, she spent as much time as possible with the child. They often went on shopping excursions to the local malls, lugging an oxygen tank along. Celine described these shopping jaunts as "get everything she wants" trips. Those expeditions ended in 1993, when Karine was sixteen. The illness had progressed and she was by then confined to her bed, barely able to breathe or swallow.

Celine remembers her final visit to Karine. "I had her in my arms," she says, "and I started to sing softly in her ear, and out of nowhere her eyes closed. I looked to my mom, who was massaging her feet because her circulation didn't work, and nodded, 'Okay, it's happening.'

One tear came down Karine's cheek, and then she went."

Karine's death greatly affected Celine. She has said that she felt like a "failure" for years after Karine's passing because she had promised her niece that everything would be okay. "Karine trusted me, believed in me so much because I kept saying all the time, 'We'll cure it,' " Celine says with sadness in her voice. "She let go and died in my arms. . . . But she is still fighting with me. I will not let her down." Devastated by the loss, Celine decided to parlay her fame and influence to do some good. Since that terrible day in 1993 she has stepped up her efforts to find a cure for the ailment.

"I love Karine very much, she's still with me," she announced in 1997. She kept Karine's memory alive by performing dozens of concerts for CF, raising hundreds of thousands of dollars for the cause. In 1993 she became a celebrity patron for the Canadian Cystic Fibrosis Foundation. "We're not playing a game, we need a cure," she said. This is no passing fancy. Celine is really committed to the cause. She has dedicated an album, *Pour Que Tu M'Aime Encore,* to her Karine, and in 1997 she brought down the house on *The Oprah Winfrey Show* when she sang a poignant song from the album in honor of her late niece. Winfrey was so overcome with emotion, she had to break for commercial to compose herself. The album and song raised a great deal of money for cystic fibrosis, and Celine continues to devote herself unselfishly to the cause.

"I always wanted to be involved to help other people," she said. "I feel good about the fact I know I'm going to be helping with my songs."

*   *   *

In the fall of 1993, at the press launch for *The Color of My Love*, Celine announced that she and René were engaged and would tie the knot in Montreal in 1994. The liner notes to that album contain a testimony of love for René. She wrote that their love was "our special dream locked away inside my heart."

"It's true," she told reporters at the press conference. "I love René and he loves me and we hope to get married within a year. I can't keep it a secret any longer."

The secret was out. Now the wedding preparations could begin.

CHAPTER NINE

◆

The Royal Wedding

FOR CELINE DION dreams do come true. From her earliest days spent daydreaming about a career as a singer, she has displayed an ability to take the ideas in her head and turn them into reality. Her wedding was no different. As a little girl she had imagined a lavish fairytale ceremony. On December 17, 1994, after a year of careful planning, Celine wed René in the kind of service usually reserved for royalty.

It was Celine's first trip down the aisle; René, however, had been married twice, and those unions produced three children. The pair were able to be married in a grand Catholic ceremony because his first marriage was nullified and his second marriage wasn't performed in a church and therefore didn't present a religious obstacle.

"I believe their intentions are serious," said the pastor of Notre Dame Basilica, Monsignor Ivanhoe Poirier, "not only because of what they've said, but because of their actions. . . . Maybe because both of them come from Catholic families and are grounded in their faith. I'm convinced that they are honest, down-to-earth, and receptive. . . . We didn't make any formal inquiry," he

79

added. "We are neither psychologists nor psychiatrists. But their relationship isn't frivolous and it seems solid."

It was planned to be Montreal's social event of the decade. Celine made every effort to keep the wedding as intimate as possible, but with such a large family it was a tough task.

"I've got thirteen brothers and sisters—I'm the fourteenth—and I'm still the baby of the family," she said while trying to put together a guest list for the wedding. "With my brothers and sisters, I have about thirty-five nieces and nephews. That's just my family, not cousins and friends, and it's about a hundred people. I have friends in show business and [people] who helped me when I started, when I wanted to be a singer—a lot of important people. I really kept this as intimate as possible and we're up to five hundred people!"

Following the March 30, 1993, engagement, five hundred of Celine and René's friends and associates were sent embossed invitations that read:

"Celine Dion and René Angelil would be happy to share this very special day with you Saturday, December 17th 1994. You are invited to attend the wedding ceremony to be held at 3:00 P.M. Notre Dame Basilica, 110 Notre Dame Street, West Montreal. A reception will follow at the Westin Mount-Royal Hotel, 1050 Sherbrooke Street West. Tuxedo. Long Dress."

Almost immediately the media jumped on the story. Trying in vain to dig up some scandal, several tabloids harped on the age difference between the couple. One weekly crime rag, *Photo Police,* ran a provocative story with the headline PUNISHABLE BY TWO YEARS IN PRISON superimposed over a photo of the couple. The front-page story implied that Celine and René had lived together before she was eighteen years old, an offense under Quebec law.

The couple's reaction was swift. A $20 million lawsuit was filed against Les Éditions du Boise Inc., the publishing house that produced the weekly newspaper. Celine's mother also filed suit. Having recently signed a deal to produce pâté and other products with Maple Leaf Foods, Thérèse maintained that the adverse publicity could hurt her professional reputation. In papers filed in court, lawyers reported that Celine and René didn't start living together until March 1993, the date of their engagement. René's lawyers and *Photo Police* eventually reached an out-of-court settlement in August 1997, which required the tabloid to print a retraction and make a donation to the Cystic Fibrosis Foundation of Quebec.

René admitted to a reporter that he was concerned about what people would think about their romance, which went from professional to personal when Celine was twenty-one. The singer was less guarded. "When you're in love, you want to scream it to the world," she said. "René has been my manager for fifteen years. He is the only man of my life, I don't know anything else. With other people, they haven't been all their lives together. Me, I don't know anything else. I can't imagine having another husband or manager. I am perfectly happy."

Other press reports were more congratulatory. "Rest assured, it will be a wedding!" roared Montreal's *La Presse*. "More than a wedding, an event; more than an event, a communion. For it isn't only Mama Dion who is marrying off a daughter. It's all of Quebec."

Once their secret was out, wedding preparations started in earnest. They booked the 170-year-old Notre Dame Basilica, the most famous Catholic church in Canada, for the December ceremony. Located in the old section of Montreal, it is a grand structure, perfect for the lavish service Celine had planned.

The design of the dress was a closely guarded secret. After fruitless searches for a designer in New York and Paris, Montreal bridal designers Mirella and Steve Gentile, owners of Bella di Serra, were chosen for the job. Their friends Della and Tony Meti are tight with Celine and René. When the Metis heard of the difficulty in finding a bridal designer, they suggested that René call the Gentiles. The first phone call came from the Dion home in Florida. At first Steve Gentile thought it was a joke.

"Celine wants a fairy-tale wedding," said René on the line. "Do what it takes to make her happy."

Once Gentile realized the phone call was not a prank, the designers went to work. A meeting was set up with Celine, who arrived with sketches and ideas. Mirella Gentile remembers the singer saying she wanted "a princess dress," a full-skirted, romantic gown. Money was no object. The singer and the designer had a meeting of minds, conjuring up a small-waisted, crinolined gown with a tight bodice, a thirty-foot train, and a curved décolletage designed to show a little cleavage. The *Montreal Gazette* wrote that "with the designer's cut, Dion's 23-inch waistline looked like 19, reinforcing the singer's idea of an Age of Innocence style."

A muslin mockup of the proposed dress was used for fittings. Once the dress had been fitted to Celine's

Lisa Rose/Globe

Celine at the 1998 Academy Awards

James M. Kelly/Globe

At Ford's Theatre Gala with the Clintons, 1994

John Barrett/Globe

Celine and René at New York Knicks/Chicago Bulls game (that's Michael Douglas), 1997

Friends

Having fun with some of the *Sesame Street* gang, 1997

Andrea Renault/Globe

Ron Davis/Shooting Star

Celine and Princess Stephanie of Monaco, 1996

Mark Allen/Globe

Concert at
Wembley, London

Celine was a
winner at the
1996 World
Music Awards,
Monte Carlo

Steve Finn/Globe

Performances

Prix Octave,
Montreal, 1996

"Top of the Pops"
BBC-TV, 1997

Celine

Celine and René Angelil
Notre Dame Basilica, Montreal
December 17, 1994

& René

Mary Monaco/Shooting Star

Ron Davis/Shooting Star

model's figure and subtle changes had been made, the Gentiles went to work sewing the garment. Approximately one thousand hours of work went into the sewing, beading, and pearling of the gown, which was made of fine Italian silk and French lace. Seamstresses worked tirelessly on the fan-shaped sleeves, two thirty-foot trains (one detachable), and long veil. Topping off the outfit was a headdress of two thousand Austrian crystals strung over a wooden frame. The piece, another of Mirella's designs, weighed seven pounds.

Mirella also designed matching dresses for the bridesmaids. Newspaper reports placed the price tag for the matching wedding-party dresses at $100,000.

The final fitting on Celine's gown occurred on December 15 at noon, two days before the wedding. The thirteen seamstresses and embroiderers worked round the clock from that point on to finish the dress for the Saturday nuptials. Many of them slept at the store, but they were able to deliver the completed gown at 1:30 A.M. on the day of the wedding. "Normally, we are not finishing a wedding dress in the middle of the night," said Steve Gentile. "We are used to doing big lineups, but this was different. It was very special for us. She's more than Quebec's daughter, she's Canada's daughter."

Since this was a winter wedding, a warm outer jacket would be required for the walk from the car to the church. Five top Montreal designers vied for the honor of creating a fur coat for Celine to wear on her wedding day. Emerging victorious was Zuki, a top designer whose fur fashions are favored by movie stars and jet-setters.

"It's a thirty-five-skin white mink jacket with very full sleeves to accommodate the wedding dress," said Zuki.

"The scalloped sleeve has a sixty-two-inch circumference. The jacket also had to be quite short, stopping just above the waistline, because the skirt of her dress was so enormous."

As with the design of her dress, Celine worked with Zuki to create her wedding jacket. He faxed a sketch of the original design to Celine when she was on tour in Tokyo. She requested a higher collar at the neck to protect her throat. "I added a little ripple," he said, "a tulip effect at the neck." Meanwhile, Dion and her hairdresser, Louis Hechter of Salon Orbite, ordered several braided hairpieces from Paris for use under the weighty headdress.

Between the Asian tour and wedding preparations, René feared Celine was doing too much. "I'm not burned out but I'm very, very tired," she said. "Sometimes I lose track of things I want to do and I want to do more, but when it gets too much, René stops me."

In the midst of all the planning and touring Celine added another jewel to her crown. She was honored with a diamond record to mark Canadian sales of over one million copies of *The Color of My Love*. Celine was only the fourth Canadian artist to sell a million records in his or her own country, and the first from Quebec.

"I didn't expect any of this," she said at a news conference. Dressed in a black suit and a purple blouse, she greeted the press and posed for hundreds of photographs. "The first time I saw something like this it had Michael Jackson's name on it. I can't believe it."

As she cradled the diamond record in her arms, she tried to put her emotions into words. "It's a great feeling, but I feel a lot of pressure," she said excitedly, the words tumbling from her mouth. "I've always felt pressure to beat my last performance, to do my best. I know I want to do this again."

René piped up, adding, "To see that she's one of the biggest stars in the world, it just goes to show that anything is possible if you believe in it. I don't know what we're going to do for an encore."

With the wedding day approaching, the legal battles persisted. As the suit against *Photo Police* was being dragged through the court, another legal action threatened to mar Celine's big day. In a move to offset the reported $500,000 cost of the wedding, René sold the exclusive rights for photographs and wedding coverage to prominent Quebec gossip magazine *7 jours*. In a deal valued at $200,000, *7 jours* was guaranteed private access to the couple and bridal party, thereby prohibiting all other newspapers and magazines from taking photos inside the church.

In answer to the ban, another French company, publishing colossus Québecor, Inc., which owns the daily tabloid *Le Journal de Montréal*, went to court to challenge *7 jours'* exclusive access. Their suit was double-pronged, at once alleging that René was interfering with the freedom of the press and that the ban broke church law, which requires all weddings to be held in public. The Québecor suit was settled just six hours before the wedding was to take place, with a judge upholding the couple's right to keep uninvited reporters and photographers from entering the church.

Despite the press ban, the wedding was the most-talked-about event in Montreal for the months leading up to the big day. Radio stations put "The Power of Love," the song Celine dedicated to René, in high rotation. Newspaper coverage was relentless. BIGGER THAN GRETZKY'S screamed one headline, referring to the celebrity wedding of Wayne Gretzky and Janet Jones six years previously in Edmonton. The tabloids reported on the guest list, who would and wouldn't be attending. They related that the much-publicized big names—Michael Jackson, Michael Bolton, Elizabeth Taylor, Barbra Streisand, Mariah Carey, and U.S. President Bill Clinton—wouldn't be attending, but former Canadian Prime Minister Brian Mulroney and his wife Mila would.

They speculated on the cost of the ceremony and what Celine would wear. It was as big a media frenzy as Montreal had ever seen. Commenting on the wedding hype, *The Toronto Star* said, "There was so much pre-wedding hype in the Quebec media that even Angelil—a show business veteran who is credited with having packaged Dion into a multi-million-dollar industry—was surprised."

Days before the wedding Celine shared her eagerness about her upcoming nuptials with a Toronto reporter. "If you asked me ten years ago," she said, "I'd say that being a singer was all that mattered to me. But today, being happy is all that matters. I'm getting married December 17, and that's what is really important.

"Everything for that day is ready. It's going to happen. To tell you the truth, it's the day after that I'm waiting for. I'm going to go on vacation with my husband and we're not going to talk showbiz at all."

Security the day of the "mega-marriage" was tight. In an effort to keep out curiosity seekers and unwanted photographers, strict instructions were issued to the invited guests. They were to report to the Westin Hotel in Montreal to receive a pass, and then board a bus that would transport them to the church. On the bus many of the guests reread and studied the instruction sheet that had been included with their invitations. It read as follows:

We are happy to know that you are joining us on Saturday, Dec. 17.

No doubt you realize that this is not an ordinary wedding, meaning that you will have to deal with a very special security plan.

Guests, reporters and staff will be clearly identified by us so that no one will attend the reception if not properly authorized.

As a guest, we kindly ask you to be at the bar of the Westin Hotel between noon and 1 o'clock for a coffee-croissant. Our reception committee will give you and your escort a special identification card that you will have to carry on you at all times during that day. It will be the key to all access and reception areas.

The basilica access being blocked for the occasion by the Montreal police department, special deluxe coaches will provide transportation for all guests, allowing them to leave their cars at the hotel parking lot. The departure is scheduled for 1:45 P.M. After the ceremony, the coaches will drive the guests back to the hotel for the reception. . . .

* * *

The instruction sheet continued with suggestions of places where guests could get their hair done and receive a 30 percent discount on tuxedo rentals. In addition, guests were directed to make contributions to the Cystic Fibrosis Foundation in lieu of wedding gifts.

In closing, the note read, "We are certain that this day full of magic will be engraved in your memories."

The day of the wedding Celine prepared by doing her own makeup, assisted by makeup artist Loretta Chiesa. A team of dressers helped her into the $25,000 gown, capping the outfit with the seven-pound headdress. She saw news reports that huge crowds were gathering outside Notre Dame Basilica to watch her entrance. Newspaper reports estimated that four hundred to five hundred people braved the bad weather to catch a glimpse of their idol. "I hope he [René] will find me beautiful," she said as they left for the church.

The five hundred invited guests arrived via six buses and several limousines half an hour before Celine's brown Rolls-Royce pulled up in front of the church. The wedding party were all driven in Rolls-Royces instead of the conventional stretch limousines. Celine was greeted by an adoring public who screamed their love for her.

"Celine! Our Cinderella," yelled one fan.

"You are our little queen!" said another, tossing a bouquet of flowers to the bride-to-be.

Flanked by her sister Ghislaine and niece Audry, the flower girl, Celine walked up the historic steps of the basilica to be greeted by her bridesmaids, her seven other sisters, who took hold of her train and prepared her for the walk down the aisle. The orchestra played the title track from *The Color of My Love* as they made their way to the altar. René waited at the front of the church, surrounded by his eight best men. Celine joined René at the altar, wiping a tear away from her cheek with a handkerchief borrowed from her father.

"You look so beautiful," said Adhemar as he handed her the handkerchief.

The solemn proceedings were broken by moments of levity. Celine curtsied and a wide smile showed on her face as René placed the wedding ring on her finger. She held up the ring for all to see, elated to finally realize her dream of being married to René. At the end of the ceremony the Montreal Jubilation Choir sang "Glory Train," and an elated Celine danced, clapping her hands above her head to the joyous music. "She looked so amazing in the gown and with her makeup," said her brother Paul. "I never saw her look more beautiful."

After the ceremony the guests were shipped off to the Montreal Westin Hotel for a press conference and reception. At the twenty-minute question-and-answer period with the press, Celine joked and parried with reporters, barely able to contain her glee.

One newspaperman asked about the dress. "I wanted the dress of a princess. Like the one we dream of in our dreams, but I'm paying the price for it today because it is not easy to get around with this. It's very heavy," she said, adding, "But I'm happy to do it, especially for you, René, because I love you so much."

She giggled when asked what she remembered about the ceremony, barely an hour before. "I remember saying yes," she said with a laugh, looking lovingly at the tuxedo-clad René. She then gave her husband three kisses and pretended to faint into his arms. "With those three kisses," wrote Sandro Contenta of *The Toronto Star*, "the public portion of the most talked about wedding in Quebec history came to pass." The press conference was over, and it was time to join the invited guests in the hotel's ballroom for the reception.

Festivities were already under way, with magicians roving from table to table, when Celine and René arrived at eight-thirty. Some guests passed the time at gaming tables, playing with cards embossed with the couple's "CR" monogram. On the dance floor Celine twirled and spun, allowing her dress to spread out, making her look, as one guest said, like "a magnificent dancing swan."

On a more serious note Celine and René used the reception as an opportunity to make a large donation to the Cystic Fibrosis Foundation. After that presentation Celine's thirteen brothers and sisters honored her by singing a song they had written especially for the occasion. She wept as she hugged them, thanking them for their musical gift.

Long after the five-course champagne dinner was over, caterers wheeled out the wedding cake. London's *Daily Mirror* described it as "an alarming 12-foot-high pyramid of profiteroles." After posing for a few photographs that showed them nibbling on cake, the couple moved next door to an adjoining room that had been set up as a casino. Using fake money, the newlyweds and guests gambled for a time before the party ended.

It had been a long day, but one that turned out just the way Celine had always dreamed it would. "It was magic," she said.

The next day the newlyweds and the Dion family celebrated Christmas—a week early—with a brunch before Celine and René left for their honeymoon at their new home in West Palm Beach, Florida. "I'm going to go there and do some cooking and cleaning and just relax and do other things," said Celine.

Just days after the wedding, *7 jours* released a 400,000-copy limited-run edition of a glossy souvenir wedding album. Priced at $6.95, the book sold out in a matter of hours, with one shopkeeper saying it "sold faster than lottery tickets on a million-dollar jackpot day."

CHAPTER TEN

————————————◆

Married Life

CELINE AND RENÉ bought a home in exclusive West Palm Beach in the early 1990s. After their honeymoon they purchased a $750,000 plot of land in nearby Jupiter. Their publicity-shy neighbors on the eight-mile-long, half-mile-wide island, 20 miles north of Palm Beach, include actor Tom Cruise and former baseball star Mike Schmidt. As Celine's star began to rise in the world market, the pair found themselves in need of a private retreat. Montreal was too hot for Celine; she couldn't go anywhere without being recognized. Florida provided a safe haven where she could relax and play golf, unencumbered by the glaring eye of the press.

The superstar's Floridian life is simple. Celine likes to keep house, cleaning, doing laundry, making beds, and cooking—"usually trying to make leftovers look better," she says, laughing. She adds that she doesn't have to do all this housework, but does it "because I like it."

Like many newlyweds René and Celine planned on starting a family. As the youngest of fourteen, Celine longs to have a brood of her own, but the demands of a show-business career and her history of irregular periods have made this difficult. In typical good humor Celine concedes that while it is taking a long time to get pregnant, she and René "are having a wonderful time trying."

In a television interview Celine shed some light on her desire to start a family. "I might be a little afraid of being the youngest and losing the people around me that are supporting me," she said candidly. She adds that having a child is the best way "to make this love last as long as possible."

She admits that while she is surrounded by family, she has few close friends. "Personal friends, to go out with, buddies . . . I do not . . . have friends like that." There isn't a trace of self-pity in her voice when she makes that admission; she is self-assured and happy with her life. "But without close pals," asked one interviewer, "who [do you] turn to when [you've] had a fight with René?"

"I don't talk to anyone about it," Celine replied. "We're two adults and we can fix our own problems. When we fight, he has a hard head, and so do I."

Like most married couples, Celine and René do argue, but are committed to one another and always find a way to resolve their differences. One spat revolved around René's obsessive use of the telephone. Like many high-powered show-business executives, he has a love affair with the telephone. It was a habit that drove Celine to distraction. "He's talking about me," she said with a hint of exasperation in her voice, "but I'd rather he talk *to* me."

After several failed attempts at separating her husband from the telephone, Celine left for a monthlong tour of Australia. Some clichés are clichés because they are true, and in this case absence made the heart grow fonder. René missed her so much, he made her a promise: when she came back home, he said, "It'll just be the two of us. No phones."

While Celine has spoken of their minor marital difficulties to the press, she is also quick to praise her husband. "René is very intense . . . and very sensitive," she says. "When he sees something beautiful or sad, he cries. But he also keeps a lot of things inside. When nervous, he eats. I would love him to lose pounds, but not for his looks, 'cause I love him that way. His belly is my own little pillow."

With marriage came a new sense of priorities for Celine. In earlier interviews she stressed the importance of hard work and career; now her tune had changed. "I used to dream of becoming a singer," she says. "Today my dream is to be healthy and happy."

Part of the plan to be happy involved creating a suitable home. In the summer of 1997 the couple began building a house on their plot of land in Jupiter. Located on Florida's Admiral Coast, the land overlooks the Atlantic Ocean on one side and the Loxahatchee River on the other. When completed, the 18,000-square-foot mansion will have fountains, waterfalls, sixty-three television sets, and enough closet space for all her clothes and several hundred pair of shoes. "She always buys two pairs," says brother Michel, "because if she broke one, she'd have another one exactly the same." The renovations will cost $8 million. The house is located near the swank Jupiter Island Club, a country club where Celine enjoys playing golf.

She first started playing golf in the summer of 1996, and as usual she set high goals for herself. The first day on the links she told René that she wouldn't be happy until she shot a double-bogey round of 108. Six weeks later, shooting 250 practice balls a day, she was almost there. "Cooking, golfing, singing—she is a perfectionist," says René with obvious admiration in his voice. "This is the only way for her."

"It's a very difficult sport," says Celine, who admits to being a perfectionist. "That little ball looks easy to hit, but it's not easy. It's very technical."

Back to business. During the periods leading up to and immediately following the wedding, Celine stayed busy. Sony released three French-language albums, 1993's *Les Premières Années compilation*, 1994's *Celine Dion à l'Olympia*, and 1995's *D'eux* (released in the U.S. under the name *The French Album*). She performed at the inauguration of President Bill Clinton singing live for thousands of enraptured fans.

D'eux was a significant album for Celine. Following the worldwide success of *The Color of My Love* and the British success of "Think Twice," *D'eux* became the best-selling French record in British history. A single, "Tu m'aimes encore" even snuck up the U.K. charts, hitting number seven. The success of that single was very pleasing for Celine, as very few French songs have done well in Britain. There have been exceptions—"Je t'aime" by Serge Gainsbourg and Jane Birkin was a hit in 1969, as were Plastic Bertrand's "Ça plane pour moi," and "Joe le taxi," Vanessa Paradis's 1988 single.

Composed by French superstar Jean-Jacques Goldman,

a man often called the "Bruce Springsteen of France," *D'eux* encompasses many styles, from folk to pop to jazz to soul. Celine shows uncommon (even for her) passion in these songs, so much so that even she was surprised. "To be face-to-face with your own emotions is pretty amazing," she said of the recording process.

When the album became the biggest-selling record ever in France (earning the distinguished Medal of Arts from the French government), it was incontrovertible proof that Celine had become, as *Time* magazine later called her, a global diva. "Diva means goddess," wrote Richard Corliss in *Time*. "The dictionary definition is more modern: 'an operatic prima donna.' Let's fiddle a little with those words. 'Operatic': note the strenuous, hyperemotional, aria-like feel to many pop ballads. 'Prima donna': to remove its suggestion of imperious temperament and translate it literally as first lady. Voila! Celine Dion . . ."

Even the Japanese succumbed to her charms. Celine set another chart record, only this time with a song that most North Americans never got the chance to hear. "To Love You More," a tune written for the Japanese television drama series *Koibito yo (My Dear Lover)*, sold 1.3 million copies in Japan, making it the first foreign song to reach the top of the charts in that country in twelve years. "To Love You More" stayed near the top of the charts for almost one full year.

Although the tune was a huge hit in Japan, "To Love You More" has its roots firmly planted in Celine's Canadian soil. Written by British Columbia–born producer David Foster and Junior Miles (the pen name of Edgar Bronfman, Jr., chairman of The Seagram Company), "To

Love You More" is destined to become a collector's item, as it has never been included on any of Celine's long-playing recordings in the Western world.

Fresh from this last round of success, Celine also began to explore the creative side of her craft. Celine the songbird was about to become Celine the songwriter. "Throughout my career," she told columnist Marilyn Beck, "people have said, 'Celine, you should write some songs' and I said, 'Forget it. It's two different careers'— singing and writing." During her mini-vacation immediately following the wedding, however, she became interested in writing.

"Because I had empty spaces and moments for the first time in my life, I started having these beautiful ideas about songs," she said, adding, "I've been calling my answering machine at home and singing a few notes to listen back to later."

She was experimenting with songwriting, but didn't feel comfortable enough to present her work to her producers. So when it came time to put together the next English-language album, the first order of business was to filter through the hundreds of songs that had been submitted for her approval.

CHAPTER ELEVEN

◇

Falling into You

THE BIG STORY surrounding the making of *Falling into You* actually dates back to October 1994. Reclusive producer Phil Spector was up late one night flipping through the channels. Spector watches a great deal of television. He compulsively studies MTV, watching and rating the videos, trying to keep up on the latest trends in music.

That fall night a young singer from Canada caught his eye. Celine was appearing on *Late Night with David Letterman*, singing a song that Spector knew very well.

In a business that hands out platitudes like they were candy at Halloween, Phil Spector truly does deserve the title of rock-and-roll royalty. As the creator of a lavish production technique known as the Wall of Sound, he is arguably the most distinctive producer in music history. In his heyday Spector was described as a genius, his music as Wagnerian. In the last decade or so, during his self-imposed semiretirement, he has more often been characterized as eccentric and egocentric.

His behavior had grown increasingly erratic over the years. Always an autocrat in the studio, even in the early days, Spector's recent studio work has been marred by some bizarre incidents. According to Mark Ribowski's book *He's a Rebel—The Truth About Phil Spector—Rock and Roll's Legendary Madman*, after seeing the Ramones at the Whiskey à Go-Go in 1980, he offered his services to the punk band, reportedly saying, "Do you want to make a good album by yourselves or a great album with me?" Jumping at the chance to work with the renowned producer, the group spent the next seven months recording *End of the Century*. The sessions were fraught with tension. One night Spector allegedly pulled a gun on drummer Dee Dee in an effort to convince him to cooperate.

To be fair to Mr. Spector, the tumultuous sessions produced the Ramones' best recorded work, earning praise for both the band and the producer. *Rolling Stone*'s Kurt Loder called it "the most commercially credible album the Ramones have ever made [and] also Phil Spector's finest and most mature effort in years." *End of the Century* was Spector's last major production for sixteen years. Several attempts to record with new bands were eventually aborted, and no new material from Spector surfaced in the eighties or nineties.

That October night he saw someone who intrigued him. Someone that might make it worth going back to the studio. Celine was singing "River Deep–Mountain High," a tune he had recorded with Tina Turner way back in 1966. Turner's version of the tune is a classic, frequently ranked in the top ten rock songs of all time.

As with the Ramones, Spector pushed Turner almost to the limit until he got the vocal he was looking for. The night they recorded the vocal track he made her sing the tune over and over until long after midnight. By the time he was satisfied, Turner was dripping with sweat, stripped down to her bra, veins bulging in her neck. Only then did Spector get what he was after—emotion laid bare.

Watching Celine belt out the song brought back memories for Spector. Here was that rare kind of singer who could uncover a song's true passion, could dig deep and bring that indescribable *something* to a song. Celine didn't have the gut-wrenching soul of Tina Turner; she was more controlled, not as wild. Spector wondered if he could loosen her up, and do something truly magical and soulful in the studio with her voice.

Celine's appearance on the Letterman show served as an audition for Spector. He decided then and there that he wanted to produce her next record, that it would be his triumphant comeback. He sent feelers out to Sony Music, making it known that he was willing to collaborate with their artist, but only if he had total control over the sessions. Sony leaped at the chance to pair up the legendary producer and their newest singing star. Around the Sony offices the matchup became known as the "dream team." Expectations were high.

Spector was to be only one of seven producers brought on board to handle Celine's new album. To raise interest in *Falling into You*, Sony concocted an unusual plan. Instead of hiring one producer to oversee the sessions, they pulled out all the stops and brought in an array of the world's best studio technicians—David Foster, Todd Rundgren, Jim Steinmen, Dan Hill, Aldo Nova, and Eric Carmen. It was Spector, however, who generated the most excitement. His prodigious reputation aside, the very fact that he came out of seclusion to work on this project legitimized Celine's superstardom.

It sent a message: when the most fabled producer in rock-and-roll history is willing to break a decade-long silence to work with you, you have arrived.

Spector approached the sessions with trepidation. To use an old expression, he felt that too many cooks would spoil the soup—that using too many producers would harm the project. To use Spector's own words, he felt it was obvious "that she was just being manipulated by the people around her. I knew that if I worked with her, I'd be able to bring out more of her own voice and expression."

All those concerned with the sessions would agree that they were turbulent. Spector, used to complete autonomy in the studio, clashed with Celine's handlers—René and Sony management—leading to a tense situation. To create his trademark Wall of Sound, Spector brought in dozens of musicians and a sixty-piece orchestra. The effect was overwhelming. The backing tracks were thunderous, with one instrument layered over the next, creating dramatic bed tracks for Celine to work with.

Spector considered this approach to Celine and her music innovative, and felt he was breaking new ground with the superstar. Unfortunately, not everyone agreed. Those in charge of the record felt that Celine's voice was getting lost in the Wall of Sound din, and suggested that Spector reevaluate his production. As could be expected, Spector did not react kindly to that suggestion, and stepped up his efforts to do the record his way.

When it came time to record Celine's vocals, his relationship with Sony and René had reached a fever pitch. Spector felt he was, in his own words, "making history," a record that would stand up next to his classic recordings of the 1960s. He clashed with everyone, including the other producers. The last straw came when he verbally lashed out at Celine during one turbulent session. Celine had to leave on a European tour, and with the production dragging on at a snail's pace, Spector left the project.

In a three-page statement released to *Entertainment Weekly*, Spector commented on the Dion debacle. He praised "the extraordinary talent of Ms. Celine Dion," but at the same time couldn't resist spewing some bile. "One thing they should have learned a long time ago," he wrote, "you don't tell Shakespeare what plays to write, or how to write them. You don't tell Mozart what operas to write, or how to write them. And you certainly don't tell Phil Spector what songs to write, or how to write them; or what records to produce, or how to produce them."

Spector was full of invective for the other producers on *Falling into You*, characterizing them as "amateurs, students, and bad clones of yours truly." At least one of his high-powered colleagues was strangely flattered by this insult. "I'm thrilled to be insulted by Phil Spector," said Jim Steinman. "He's my god, my idol. To be insulted by Phil Spector is a big honor. If he spits on me, I consider myself purified."

Celine publicly offered a simple explanation for the parting of ways. "We had a plan, we have to follow it. He knew about it and he didn't follow it. I cannot wait a year for him," she said, suggesting that Spector left the project because of a shortage of time to realize his vision.

Nothing from the Spector sessions was ever released.

The reclusive producer claims ownership of the tapes and vows to release them one day. He immodestly says the finished tapes "should put her [Celine] on the covers of both *Time* and *Newsweek* magazines." The unreleased tapes of the three songs sit locked in Spector's Los Angeles studio.

The Spector sessions, though aborted, generated hundreds of column inches in newspapers all over North America. One writer noted that "people do testify to the extraordinary power of [Dion's] pipes. After all, Dion is the siren who lured Phil Spector back into the studio." Even before *Falling into You* was released, it was big news.

The rest of the *Falling into You* sessions went smoothly and quickly and offered up several songs of hit-single quality. The Jim Steinman–written-and-produced "It's All Coming Back to Me Now" is a sweeping opus of almost epic proportions. Perfect for Celine, who, one writer said, has "the brash power and bravado of [Ethel] Merman with the range of Whitney Houston."

Steinman is best known for his work with rock singer Meat Loaf. In 1977 the pair teamed up to record one of the most popular records of the rock era, *Bat Out of Hell*. That record sold millions of copies, turning Meat Loaf into an international star. In the United States *Bat Out of Hell* sat on the *Billboard* album chart for an astonishing eighty-two weeks, an impressive feat dwarfed only by its success in Britain, where it became the longest-charting album of all time, staying on the charts for 450 weeks. The duo went their separate ways after that record, regrouping in 1993 for a new project called *Bat Out of Hell II: Back into Hell*. The old magic was still there, and that record produced a number-one hit with "I'd Do Anything for Love (But I Won't Do That)." It reestablished Meat Loaf as a viable star after a few lean years, while only strengthening Steinman's reputation as a hit maker.

Steinman's modus operandi rarely varies from one project to another, whether he is producing Bonnie Tyler, Meat Loaf, or Celine. He works on a grand scale, conceptualizing long intricate songs that owe more to an operatic style than to rock and roll. His original version of "I'd Do Anything for Love (But I Won't Do That)" runs more than twelve minutes, while his contribution to *Falling into You*, "It's All Coming Back to Me Now," clocks in at eight minutes; very long for a hit single.

Celine enjoyed the challenge of working with such a large palette. She reveled in the chance to get inside the song and fully explore the emotional depth of Steinman's creation. "It's like *Gone With the Wind*—it's like a movie," she said of "It's All Coming Back to Me Now."

"It's been frustrating to have a three-minute song or a four-minute song. I hate it when you have all those TV shows and they want you to do three minutes. You don't have time to get into it, it's so fast. But a song like this," she continued, "you have time to open your eyes and close them, share moments with the audience, and you have time to do something. If you love to sing, and be dramatic and romantic, this is the song for that."

Radio programmers agreed with Celine's assessment of the tune and put it in heavy rotation despite its length. Steinman also ended up producing the Spector-penned "River Deep–Mountain High," applying his usual layer of gloss to the tune. Mark Weisblott, writing in *Eye* magazine, said the updated version of the Tina

Turner song "comes off like a jungle-techno ditty with the pitch control on the fritz, at once optimistic and apocalyptic. This is the sound of the Wall of Sound being chipped away once and for all, and Celine Dion is devilishly shaking the spray can."

The last tune recorded for the record came courtesy of a movie soundtrack and writer Diane Warren. Warren was hired to provide a theme song for the Robert Redford/Michelle Pfeiffer movie *Up Close and Personal*. She saw the rough cut of the film on a Friday, and by late Saturday morning the song was finished. She says the song "just came out."

"I started to write a chorus," Warren told *Billboard*, "and the chorus lyrically and musically wrote itself." She is quick to add that she didn't write the song as a romantic love song, but as a tribute to her late father. Early on in her songwriting career, when she was discouraged by the cool reception she received from music publishers, her father cheered her on, telling her to have faith in herself. His love and belief in her talent kept her going through the lean years. "Because You Loved Me" was a daughter's way of thanking her dad.

The song was initially offered to Toni Braxton, who was looking for material to complete an album. Braxton rejected the tune, judging it to be not her style. Celine was not originally considered, because her album was already finished and the first single was set for release. Celine was familiar with Warren's work, having recorded two of her tunes in the past. The song came to Celine's attention through Polly Anthony of the 550 Music label, who was shopping Warren's demo around. Celine loved the song and agreed to record it and reshuffle her up-coming album to include the song. "Because You Loved Me" was scheduled as the first single release.

"Because You Loved Me" was featured in every television ad for the movie *Up Close and Personal*, giving Celine and the song almost round-the-clock play. Warren credits the advertising exposure with pushing the song into the number-one spot, as well as turning Celine into a household name. "That's once-in-a-lifetime exposure for an artist," she says.

It could have remained at number one on the Hot 100 for longer than six weeks if you believe America Online's insider gossip Web site *The Velvet Rope*. They charged that Sony Music, Celine's label, pulled "Because You Loved Me" off the market so that Mariah Carey, the other Sony Music diva, could take the number-one spot unchallenged. As the remaining stock of "Because You Loved Me" disappeared from stores, reported sales of the song dropped 24 percent, enough to allow Carey's "Always Be My Baby" to take over the top spot.

Some industry insiders said that pulling Celine's single was a perfectly reasonable thing to do so that sales of the single wouldn't hurt the sales of *Falling into You*. Others were more suspicious. It was noted that Carey was then married to Sony Music president Tommy Mottola, the only man at Sony with enough power to order such a move. Sony Music has never officially responded to the charge that Mottola used his influence to advance his wife's career.

The discontinuation of "Because You Loved Me" didn't dampen the public's appetite for the song—it reigned over the Hot 100 for six weeks, but did even better on the *Billboard* Adult Contemporary chart, holding fast at number one for a record-breaking nineteen weeks.

At this time Celine broke new ground. She became the first Canadian with her own prepaid phone card. A photo of Celine appears on the Bell Hello phone card, which enables customers to make long-distance calls after punching in a personal identification number. The thing that distinguishes this card from others on the market is the access it offers to the singing star.

Users of the card are able to access a series of taped messages from Celine talking about her favorite subjects, including her music, family, and shopping habits. "I love high-heel shoes," she says in one message. "They're very feminine and sexy and you walk differently than when you wear running shoes." Another message describes her home life: "I love cooking and cleaning and being around in my house with René, my husband. Being in our pool together. Just spending time together."

Cardholders are invited to leave personal messages for Celine, although she won't be returning any of the calls. "I doubt that she'll actually sit and listen to the messages," said Stentor phone alliance representative Salvatore Iacono. "She has people who do that for her."

The cards are available in denominations of $10, $20, $50, $75, and $100 and may be ordered through a special sales line, 1-800-555-DION. One dollar from the sale of each card goes to the Canadian Cystic Fibrosis Foundation.

* * *

With a new album soon to be in the stores, Celine's management arranged dozens of interviews and press conferences. By this time she was a big star and would have to face tougher questions from reporters. They would not be satisfied talking only about the music. Not now; she was too big. This time the questions would be of a more personal nature.

Her hometown press—reporters from Montreal— were the hardest hitting. Celine did her best to be gracious and answer the personal questions in an up-front and truthful way. She told the media at one press junket in Montreal that she wouldn't be taking a planned "sabbatical year" because she wasn't pregnant. "There's still a lot of time to have children, even if it's not this year," she said.

One topic, however, that she didn't talk about publicly was the rumor that she was anorexic. It was unsubstantiated gossip that had been circulating in the Quebec and U.S. tabloids, usually accompanied by an unflattering candid photo of Celine. One salient point these sensational stories always failed to mention was Celine's family history. Sure, she was thin—and had been told by several doctors to put on weight—but so was her father, Adhemar. Adhemar was always in fine health, even though he was underweight. This inherited trait, coupled with her punishing work schedule, made it difficult for Celine to put on weight. Her family often jokes that if it wasn't for Thérèse's rich French food, Adhemar would weigh even less than he does now.

By all reports Celine has a normal appetite and often even enjoys dessert after dinner. Her svelte figure, then, can be attributed to plenty of exercise (she enjoys golf, swimming, and tennis) and the activity of a heavy workload.

Falling into You was released in March 1996 to good reviews. *Billboard* magazine called it "a deep album that will solidify Dion's reputation as one of the world's true pop divas," while *RPM* magazine said, "The point here is, there's really not much need for criticism, because it would be fruitless. This album will sell a ton, and with a voice like that, she deserves every penny." *Falling into You* debuted at the number-two position on the *Billboard* charts, held out of the top spot by a fellow Canadian, Alanis Morisette. Worldwide, it smashed records, reaching the top spot on the charts in France, England, Switzerland, Belgium, the Netherlands, Norway, Austria, and Australia. It seemed nobody was immune to Celine's charms.

Everyone seemed to have an opinion on how Celine should proceed now that she was at the top. Bruce Allen, the outspoken manager of Bryan Adams, was concerned that she might become overexposed. Adams had released only six studio albums in the course of his career versus the eight albums Celine produced in the 1990s alone.

"It's great if you can wait it out," Allen told the *Calgary Herald*. "Adams takes three or four years between albums, and I think that's why he still has a career. The danger is putting out too many too quick. Too much product is a problem. As good as Celine is, the public can get tired of her."

Allen blames record companies who pressure artists

to produce and make money today with little concern for the long term. "All these companies are on the acquisition trail and they have to pay down their debt," he says. "The pressure is ridiculous. You have to stand up and not react. René holds all the cards. She is the five-hundred-pound gorilla. She sings when she wants to sing. You gotta be confident. You've got to leave the public wanting more."

A close friend of René's disagrees with Allen's assessment. "I don't think it will stop, because they're perfectionists," says Pierre Lacroix, general manager of the Colorado Avalanche hockey team. "Everything they've done is with a vision and he's had a great vision since day one. He makes the right calls at every stage."

CHAPTER TWELVE

---◆---

Olympic Gold

JULY OF 1996 saw Celine reach her biggest audience ever. She was used to performing in front of large crowds, but by accepting an invitation to sing at the opening ceremonies of the Atlanta Olympic Games, she would be hitting new heights. "Three billion people watching is pretty frightening," she said. "This moment is coming very fast now, and I have goose bumps."

The opening ceremonies were planned to be a spectacle rarely seen on television. Here's how the numbers break down. The three-and-a-half-hour long show featured 5,500 performers (including Celine, Gladys Knight, and John Williams conducting the Atlanta Symphony Orchestra), playing to a live crowd of 83,100. Stage-managing the enormous show required 2,100 backstage personnel and 650 field marshals. It took 35 people to launch the 5,000 fireworks that lit up the sky over the Olympic Stadium. That's enough fireworks to fill three eighteen-wheel trucks. Lighting for the show was provided by 322 people, operating 110 7,000-watt Xenon lights designed especially for the ceremony, 270 Veralights, 38 spotlights, 3,000 incandescent lights, and 16,000 household-style lightbulbs. Sewing the costumes for the more than 5,000 extras involved in the performance took 56,200 man-hours and used 61,000 yards (55,800 meters) of fabric and 1.6 million sequins. The spectacular field cover used during the ceremony was made of 27,000 square yards (22,500 square meters) of nylon mesh loomed in Lyons, France, broken down into 2,200 separate pieces joined by snaps and Velcro. Atlanta artists used 600 gallons (2,600 liters) of paint to decorate the nylon cover.

As Ed Sullivan might have said, "This was one really *big* show."

It was a steamy July night in Atlanta when the Call to Nations, a drummed invocation of the spirits of past Olympics, kicked off the Olympic centenary ceremony. Field-level temperature was in the nineties as brightly costumed dancers carried five mammoth flags of silk—in blue, yellow, green, red, and black, the colors of the Olympics—over the heads of the spectators, which included figure skater Katerina Witt, Ted Turner with his wife Jane Fonda, as well as Bruce Willis and Demi Moore.

As Grateful Dead drummer Mickey Hart led the rhythm section, the dancers formed the five interlocking Olympic rings and the numeral 100, in tribute to the Olympic centenary (the first modern games, organized by Baron Pierre de Coubertin, were held in Athens in 1896). It was an uncommonly beautiful and graceful maneuver, summing up in one fluid choreographed move the harmony and spirit so central to the games.

President Bill Clinton beamed as he made his historic opening remarks. "I declare open the games of Atlanta celebrating the Twenty-sixth Olympiad of the modern era," he said from the presidential box.

Backstage, Celine performed vocal warm-ups to prepare for her biggest show to date. She knew this was an important gig and was going to give it her all, not just for the live audience (who paid anywhere from $212 to $636 for their seats), but for the estimated 3.5 billion people watching at home. She had always been a fan of the Olympics, and greatly admired the athletes, who, like her, strove to be the best in the world. "In 1976, for a brief moment I wanted to be Nadia Comaneci," said Celine, who was only eight years old when the Olympics were held in her home province of Quebec.

Following a tribute to Martin Luther King, Jr., one of Atlanta's most revered citizens, and a thrilling fireworks display, Celine took the stage. "I'll have people surrounding me, supporting me," she said, "making sure I'm not forgetting my words." She wasn't kidding. Sharing the stage with her were one hundred musicians and three hundred backup singers as she belted out a tune written especially for the opening ceremony.

"The Power of the Dream," a song by David Foster, Kenneth "Babyface" Edmonds, and Linda Thompson was commissioned for the occasion. "I was, of course, flattered and honored that they asked me five months ago to sing the song," Celine said. "To be honest with you, I didn't even think about it when they asked me. I just went for it, heard the song, and couldn't wait to sing."

Conveying the emotion of the tune was no problem for Celine, who did truly believe in the power of dreams. When she was fifteen years old, she told a reporter that she dreamed of being a star by age thirty. Now here she was at age twenty-eight with an album at the top of the world's charts, singing in front of the largest television audience ever. Watching her sing that night, one couldn't help but think that she was a true Olympian—the embodiment of talent and spirit—the best in the world. She had made her dream come true. Now that the games were open, it was the athletes' turn.

CHAPTER THIRTEEN

◇

A Doubleheader

THE EVENTS OF March 24, 1997, will forever be etched in Celine's mind. It was Hollywood's big night—the Academy Awards—and she was scheduled to perform "Because You Loved Me," the love theme from *Up Close and Personal*.

Show producer Gil Cates said the theme of 1997's Oscar show was "the experience of going to the movies. We're celebrating the togetherness aspect of it all. It's a gentler theme than we've done before. The thing that's kind of wonderful about movies is that you watch them with other people."

Film clips shown during the telecast were chosen to illustrate that the movie theater "is a wonderful place where you come together to laugh, to cry." The 1997 Academy Awards was planned as a kinder, gentler ceremony than previous shows.

Returning as master of ceremonies was Billy Crystal, taking his fifth turn as ringmaster. Crystal says he trains hard for weeks before Oscar night, and just before stepping out on stage he'll do 200 sit-ups and 150 push-ups. "I like to feel pumped up," he says. "It's like a big game."

Although Crystal's offhand style suggests that he

improvises his material, weeks of writing and careful planning actually go into his comedy bits. The script for the show is kept top secret, although Crystal promised he would avoid saying "Show me the money," the catch-phrase from *Jerry Maguire*. *New York* magazine nastily "handicapped" Crystal's monologue:

1:1 Lincoln Bedroom joke with the "Show me the money" punchline.

3:1 "You look maaaaavelous," spoken in a Minnesota accent. (A play on the accents featured in the movie *Fargo*.)

6:1 Joke about cloning the Coen brothers.

50:1 Anything either controversial or funny.

Ignoring the snarly *New York* magazine article, Crystal approached his duties with typical good humor. In a statement to the press he praised one pair of presenters. "We go way back," he said. "It means a lot to me to be working with Beavis and Butt-head. I've known them since they were pencil drawings." Scheduled to appear as presenters were Mel Gibson, Nicolas Cage, Chris O'Donnell, Jodie Foster, Kenneth Branagh, Kevin Spacey, Michael Douglas, and Helen Hunt.

The competition in the Best Song category was stiff. In addition to "Because You Loved Me," Kenny Loggins was up for "For the First Time" from the film *One Fine Day*. Loggins was no stranger to the Academy, having written and performed songs on several successful soundtracks, including *Top Gun* and *Footloose*. Madonna was set to perform *Evita*'s love ballad, "You Must Love Me," while Natalie Cole was scheduled to sing "I Finally Found Somebody" from the Barbra Streisand film *The Mirror Has Two Faces*. The song was cowritten by Canadian singer Bryan Adams (this was his third Academy Award nomination for Best Song), Streisand, Mutt Lange, and Marvin Hamlisch.

Streisand had been asked to perform the song during the ceremony, but declined, reportedly furious that *The Mirror Has Two Faces*, which she directed and starred in, had been passed over for Best Picture.

The fifth song, "That Thing You Do," from the film of the same name, would be presented as the night's big production number, with thirty-two dancers choreographed by Otis Sallid, who has worked on music videos and such films as *Do the Right Thing*.

While Celine would perform "Because You Loved Me," she was not actually nominated for an Academy Award; songwriter Diane Warren was.

The day before the Academy Awards was to air in front of an estimated one billion viewers, the unexpected happened. Natalie Cole called in sick and would not be able to perform "I Finally Found Someone." "Like everybody," says Celine, "singers get sick sometimes." Scrambling to find a replacement, the show's producers asked Celine if she would step in. She couldn't resist the opportunity to make Oscar history—no one had ever sung two songs on one broadcast before—but had one request. "I said 'I cannot learn the song by heart, but if I can have a stand with the lyrics on it, of course I would love to.'"

Celine didn't know that Barbra Streisand was going to

be in the audience that night. "Because to me," said Celine, "if she's not going to sing her song, she's not going to be there.

"So here I am walking [up the] red carpet the night of the Oscars, and everybody says, 'We just talked to Barbra,' and I said, 'Sorry, excuse me?' They said, 'Yeah, she's here.' " As if the pressure of singing a new song in front of one billion people wasn't enough, now Celine had the extra pressure of singing in front of the woman she says is one of her idols. "I'm going to sing and she's going to be seated there," she said incredulously. "No way."

Barbra or no Barbra, however, Celine was committed to sing, and since the show must go on, she took the stage. She was a vision in a low-cut sequined dress, accented by a comet-shaped Chanel neckpiece, dripping in jewels. With 656 diamonds, costing hundreds of thousands of dollars, the cometlike torque coiled around her neck, with a star lying on her upper chest and a six-pronged tail spreading down into her cleavage.

Celine scanned the audience, trying to find Streisand, to catch a glimpse of her idol. As the opening notes of "I Finally Found Someone" filled the Shrine Auditorium, Celine became lost in the song, concentrating very hard to sing every word. She couldn't see Streisand, but assumed she was sitting close to her, listening to every syllable.

Well, she wasn't. In a move that was widely reported in the press as a snub, Streisand left the auditorium just before Celine took the stage to sing "I Finally Found Someone." The tabloids had a heyday with the story. Supermarket tabloid *The Globe* reported on the story under the banner STREISAND: A STAR IS SCORNED! They reported that Streisand was "cracking under the weight of her 29-year-old rival's popularity." The hyperbolic story quotes a friend of Streisand's, who said, "She's never faced a competitor like Celine, who not only sings the same style of music so well but is much younger and prettier. Barbra is tearing her hair out!"

Of course the tabs are always looking for a juicy story, quoting unnamed sources and hyping events until they appear to be much more fantastic than they actually were. Celine has a different take on what actually happened. In conversation with Oprah Winfrey, during Oprah's series of shows from Texas in February 1998, she gave her take on the story. She acknowledges that Streisand did slip out to the bathroom during her performance, but she added sympathetically, "Oh, poor her. Well, you know, when you gotta go, you gotta go."

Celine and Oprah went on to discuss the washroom situation at these big events—the long lineups with no butting in, no matter who you are. "You are standing in line and nobody cares because they all gotta go, too. So they go, 'Barbra, you just have to wait, girl,' " said Oprah. " 'Cause that is the one place we are all equal."

Celine didn't find out until after the Academy Awards what had actually happened—that Streisand missed her performance. Several days after the event, however, Streisand sent a bouquet of flowers with a note. "She sent me a beautiful note," said Celine. "She sent me beautiful flowers and said, 'Next time, let's do one together.' "

Celine was touched by the gesture, thankful that her idol took time to make amends. She thought Streisand was just being nice, making an offer to sing together that would never come to pass. René, however, saw a business opportunity. "He took this very seriously," said Celine.

René started working the phones, tracking down David Foster (who had a long history with both Streisand and Celine), Streisand's manager, and Walter Afanasieff, urging them to make the diva duet of the decade happen.

Eventually Celine and Streisand spoke on the phone, formulating a plan for their proposed duet. Would they sing together? Would Streisand do her part first? By the end of the conversation they had worked out the details, and Celine would soon realize her dream of singing with Barbra Streisand.

Celine's choice of jewelry on Oscar night started a trend that pleased Andrea Pope, an artisan who specializes in modern torques. "People have gone ballistic; business has doubled," Pope said from her Toronto apartment. "The biggest problem I had before the Academy Awards was recognition of what my jewelry was. Now everybody knows what they are."

Pope didn't design the piece Celine wore at the Oscars, but has been making similar torques—neckpieces that derive from ancient Celtic jewelry made of metal ropes—for some time. She began making them as a lark. "I had an old piece of wire rope from a scrapyard, wrapped it around my neck, and started playing with it."

Using base metals embellished with gold, silver, and antique brass, Pope has been able to keep her prices in the affordable $40 to $150 range. "Even though Celine's cost in the hundreds of thousands of dollars, and these were obviously copies, they sold like crazy because people wanted to emulate her."

Style and clothes have always been very important to Celine. She has an acknowledged shoe fetish—she owns hundreds of pairs—and enjoys fine clothes. Since achieving international star status, she has become a client of famed couturiers Chanel, Versace, and Christian Dior. For casual wear, on the golf course, she favors Ralph Lauren.

For her live shows Celine often does her own makeup, with sister Manon managing her hair. She is very good at applying her own makeup because she has been doing it since she was a young performer. On special occasions, however, Parisian makeup artist Laura Mercier is called in. Mercier lines Dion's eyes with black pencil, applies shadows in purples, grays, or dark greens, and coats the lashes in black mascara. "She has the most beautiful eyes," says Mercier, "so we really emphasize them." Mercier rounds out Celine's face with Rose Petal blush and natural beige-and-pink tones on her lips. The finished look is capped with a few spritzes of Chanel No. 5, Celine's favorite perfume.

Nineteen ninety-seven was the year the Grammys honored one very famous American, tried to correct an old slight, and handed out sixteen nominations to Canadians, including four to Celine.

Hillary Rodham Clinton was the unanticipated winner of the night. She won in the Best Spoken Word or Non-musical Album category for the audiotape of her best-selling book *It Takes a Village*. "I was very surprised because I didn't know that Grammys were given to tone-deaf people," she said backstage, while Rage Against the Machine were onstage collecting their Grammy for Best Metal Performance. Her win marked the first time a Grammy had been given to a first lady.

In an attempt to right an embarrassing wrong, the National Academy of Recording Arts and Sciences awarded three Grammys to the Beatles. The pop legends had largely been ignored by the Grammys, having won only four awards in the span of one of the most impressive careers in music history. With the release of *Anthology*, the Academy saw a chance to rewrite history and bestow the band with several more awards, bringing their career total up to seven. They won for Best Pop Performance by a Duo or Group with a Vocal for the song "Free as a Bird," which was released in 1995 but based on a two-decade-old vocal by John Lennon.

The other two awards came at the expense of Canadians. The "Free as a Bird" video beat Alanis Morisette in the Music Video Short Form category. "I hope John [Lennon] likes it," said the video's director Joe Pykta as he claimed his statue. The documentary *Anthology* also beat out Toronto-based Rhombus Media in the Best Video Long Form category.

Celine was nominated in all the key categories— Album of the Year, Pop Album of the Year (both for *Falling into You*), Record of the Year, and Best Pop Vocal Performance (for the hit "Because You Loved Me").

Early in the show, accompanied by David Foster on piano, she delivered a dramatic rendition of "Because You Loved Me," in front of the 12,000 audience members at Madison Square Garden in New York City.

Later *Falling into You* scored Best Pop Album, beating out ex-Police bassist Sting, R&B songbird Toni Braxton, and "folky" acts Tracy Chapman and Shawn Colvin.

Celine picked up her second award that night for the coveted Album of the Year. "I realize every day that talent is not enough and I want to thank everyone who works in the shadows," she said as she collected the trophy. She went on to thank her thirteen siblings and René. And "everybody in Quebec—*merci beaucoup!*"

CHAPTER FOURTEEN

———————◆———————

Let's Talk About Love

CELINE HAS BEEN honored with so many awards it would take an entire book to list them. Starting in 1982, she has collected the highest tributes the record industry has to offer.

In 1993 she became the only Canadian to win a Grammy, an Oscar, and *Billboard*, Juno, and Félix Awards in the same year. The prizes kept coming, but in 1997 she was chosen for an award that was very special for her.

Celine already had a clutch of Juno Awards. The metronome-style statuette was first awarded in a small 1971 ceremony to honor Canada's brightest and best in the recording field. Since then it has grown to become a hallmark of musical success in the Great White North. Past recipients include Anne Murray, Gordon Lightfoot, Joni Mitchell, Leonard Cohen, the Guess Who, Neil Young, and Alanis Morisette. Celine had stepped up to the Juno podium ten times, but the 1997 award was something different. This time she would share the award with two other powerful Canadian women—Alanis Morisette and Shania Twain.

Morisette was already an established star in Canada before the release of *Jagged Little Pill* transformed her into a worldwide singing sensation. Her career parallels Celine's in many ways. Born in Ottawa, Morisette has been singing since she was old enough to walk. In 1977, at the age of three, she memorized the entire score of *Grease*, and using a nail-polish bottle as a microphone often sang it in a loud clear voice for her family. Even then, she was single-minded—she wanted to feel the heat of the spotlight.

Her dream came true in 1991 with the release of a full length CD titled *Alanis*. She cowrote each of the ten dance tracks and scored a top five Canadian hit with "Too Hot." Canadian success continued with the 1992 release *Now Is the Time*, moving 100,000 units and earning a gold record. Alanis's brand of dance pop earned her the label of "the Paula Abdul of Canada."

Although successful in Canada, the first two records were not released in the United States. With an eye toward an American release, she left Ottawa and, like Celine, took an extended sabbatical to retool her image. She reemerged with *Jagged Little Pill*, and a harder-edged sound that took the world by storm. Sales of 15 million gave Alanis Morisette the all-time biggest-selling U.S. debut album by a female. It also ties her with Hootie & the Blowfish's *Cracked Rear View* as the second best-selling debut album, just behind *Boston*.

Shania Twain hails from Timmins, a small city in northern Ontario. She eked out a living as a lounge singer for several years before turning to country music. An independently released debut album showcased her impressive voice, but did little to win over country fans.

The second time is a charm, however, and the release of *The Woman in Me* saw Twain move 9 million albums from the stores. Her navel-baring crop tops and a series of sexy videos made her a country-music superstar.

These women embodied all that Canada's music industry had to celebrate. They were the Three Musketeers of Canadian music, with their latest albums selling a staggering 50 million copies worldwide. One writer noted, "Over the past 18 months, all three have vaulted over the walls of that rarely-penetrated fortress known as the US market and ascended to the ranks of musical aristocracy."

Canadian music underwent a power surge in 1996—spearheaded by these three women—which proved to be a turning point as Canadians began making serious international headway. Canadians hadn't dominated the charts for almost two decades, since the days when Joni Mitchell, Paul Anka, Neil Young, Gordon Lightfoot, the Guess Who, and Anne Murray whipped out hit after hit. One writer noted, "For a while, it seemed to be a revolving door of the same talented faces."

"Anne Murray and Gordon Lightfoot took 'em all," said musician Trevor Hurst, referring to the Juno awards.

Those days are gone. Following Celine's lead, Canadian artists were getting noticed internationally and at home. For example, in 1997, international artists earned 494 gold, platinum, and diamond records (awarded for sales of 50,000, 100,000, and one million respectively). Canadians brought in 122 gold-, platinum-, and diamond-record certifications—nearly one-fourth of the worldwide total.

The Juno commission searched for a special way to commemorate the power trio's feat. They came up with a special award—a special Juno congratulating Celine, Alanis, and Shania for international achievement. Lee Silversides, president of the Canadian Academy of Arts and Sciences, the Juno's governing body, said the three superstars "have made history around the world this year and we all watched with pride as each of these extraordinary careers unfolded."

The night of the awards only Celine and Twain were able to attend. Morisette, tired after a year of promoting *Jagged Little Pill*, was taking an extended vacation in India. Twain flew in from Nashville to accept the award. Wearing a floor-length red evening gown, she gushed as she addressed the live Juno audience. "I just can't believe it. The support in this country has been so overwhelming for me, I can't tell you how wonderful it is."

Celine's sequined blue gown shimmered as she graciously acknowledged Twain's success. "Around the world, when I travel I hear your music and it feels so good inside."

"This country is kickin' butt around the world," said a patriotic Twain as the awards ceremony came to a close. English-speaking Canada's music industry had finally, publicly acknowledged Celine's presence.

In planning Celine's next album there was just one question in the Dion camp: how can we top *Falling into You*? That record topped the charts in most of the world, selling some 25 million copies. Celine was at the summit of the mountain, so which direction should she go?

After much thought Sony decided to take Celine in a new direction for *Let's Talk About Love*, enlisting not only the world's best producers, but singers as well. Celine had never recorded a duet album in English or French, so why not bring in some other voices to spice up the mix? Contracts were drawn up with a bevy of singers to perform with her and broaden the album's marquee appeal. It was an ambitious project, bringing together Luciano Pavarotti, the Bee Gees, Carole King, and of course, Barbra Streisand.

This was an important release, not only for Celine, but for Sony as well. The Japanese-owned multinational considered *Let's Talk About Love* to be their most important commercial release of the season and threw their considerable weight behind the project. Many top-flight songwriters were asked to submit songs, including a man who was a star in his own right in Canada.

Corey Hart was born in 1957 in Quebec, and following years spent around the world—he lived in Spain, Mexico, and Florida—he settled in New York to pursue a career in music. Befriending members of Billy Joel's backup band, Hart began singing in clubs. Returning to Montreal, he signed a record deal with Aquarius Records, releasing a series of top-selling singles, including "I Wear My Sunglasses at Night," "Never Surrender," and "Can't Help Falling in Love." In the mid-eighties he was a fast-rising star whose boyish good looks led Robert Zemekis to offer him a screen test for the lead role in *Back to the Future*. In the early nineties he took a six-year-break, coming out of semiretirement to release a new record in 1997 and to work with Celine.

Hart contributed two songs to *Let's Talk About Love*,

"Miles to Go (Before I Sleep)" and "Where Is the Love?" "First and foremost, it was a great honor and a thrill to be called and asked to write for her," he says, "and then, further to that, to produce for her. I thought they would bring in some outside producers since they've got the best in the world working with her.

"But they like the way I produce, so they gave me a shot at that as well. I really enjoyed working with her," he continues. "I found her to be a delight. She's a real hard worker and she's got great natural instincts as a singer."

Hart resisted singing on the tracks himself. "As a producer I can choose the best background singers in the world and therefore wouldn't hire myself," he says with a laugh.

In the studio the pressure was intense. Sony Music Entertainment president Tommy Mottola often sat in on sessions, an unusual move for the record executive. With so much at stake, there was a great deal of scrutiny in the studio. "There were a lot of people watching," says Hart, understating the obvious.

Each year 20,000 men and women judged to have made their mark in politics, entertainment, and sports are listed in the *International Who's Who*. The English editors of the book are very exclusive about who appears in the 1,700-page volume, which has been published annually since 1935. Pamela Anderson Lee, for instance, didn't make the cut even though a worldwide Angus Reid poll stated that her name was recognized by 90 percent or more of respondents.

"Just doing *Baywatch* isn't enough," said Richard Fitzwilliams, who has edited the list of biographies for the past twenty-two years, "and the second thing is that her one film was a disaster. There's no reason at all to put her in. Simply getting a lot of media attention won't get you in the volume."

The list is revised every year and those who have sunk to obscurity are removed, as are the dead. In their place are new names, judged to be of world significance. Fitzwilliams says only two names have remained on the list since the first edition: "To promote international understanding," German film director Leni Riefenstahl (known for her Nuremberg Rally documentary *Triumph of the Will*) and King Michael of Romania, who led a coup d'état against pro-Nazi dictator Ion Antonescu in 1944. Nineteen ninety-seven saw nine hundred new names added to the roll call, including several prominent Canadians.

"In fact, there's quite a Canadian contingent," says Fitzwilliams. "Is Celine Dion not Canadian? And also Bryan Adams has Canadian connections, hasn't he? They're new. Ms. Morisette made it into the book based on the success of her last release, *Jagged Little Pill*, which sold 26 million copies worldwide. Entries have to have staying power and also a fairly significantly successful career."

Mr. Fitzwilliams was adamant that Celine belongs among the book's other famous names. "Celine Dion's *Falling into You*, of course, was a very significant album and she's had a very large body of work," he said. "We have not the first doubt that she has the staying power that it needs."

*   *   *

Everyone who worked with Celine on *Let's Talk About Love* had nothing but praise for her zeal and professionalism. Even Sir George Martin, a record producer with over four decades of experience, was wowed by his time spent with the young woman from Charlemagne. He had seen Celine on television and in shows from time to time and says he was "always enormously impressed with her. . . . I knew she could sing well, but she has the ability to put a wonderful human quality into her voice. She understands the lyrics and the emotion of it so well."

Sir George Martin is more qualified than most to pass judgment on Celine's singing ability. Starting in 1955, when he produced his first hit record at the Parlophone Studios in London, he has been one of rock's most prolific and successful recording technicians. At Parlophone he became adept at working with a wide variety of artists. Among them were ballad singers like Shirley Bassey and Matt Monroe; skiffle groups such as the Vipers; jazz bands, including Temperance 7, Johnny Dankworth, and Humphrey Lyttelton. He even produced several wildly successful comedy records for Peter Sellers.

Martin is best known for signing the Beatles to Parlophone in 1962, a relationship that lasted until the band broke up in 1970. As a talent scout it was Martin who insisted that original Beatle drummer Pete Best be let go and replaced by Ringo Starr. It was in the studio, however, that his true genius shone through. Martin devised many recording innovations—including tape loops—that set the Beatles' records apart from everything else on the charts at the time.

After the dissolution of the Beatles, Martin kept busy, opening a studio on the Caribbean Island of Montserrat. Paul McCartney, Dire Straits, and the Rolling Stones were frequent visitors to this facility, which was destroyed by a hurricane in 1989. He was knighted by Queen Elizabeth in the early nineties, enabling him to use the title "sir." Since then he has continued to remain active in music, but is selective about the projects he takes on.

In 1997, at age seventy-one, he announced his plans to retire. Then Celine came calling. Martin was asked to record "The Reason," a planned duet between Dion and legendary songwriter/singer Carole King. He leaped at the chance to record Celine, a woman he jokingly says he "was in love with."

Adding Martin to the roster of producers lent prestige to *Let's Talk About Love*—a calling card that would guarantee even heavier press coverage when the album was released. Celine says she was thrilled to work with Martin, although at first she was intimidated by him. She says she "had so much admiration for him, that I didn't know how to be." She had little to worry about because Martin was taken with her from the moment they met. They quickly formed a mutual admiration society. "Celine was a hero and became a friend," said Martin. For her part, Celine heaped praise on the legendary producer. "I feel . . . he is a diamond," she said, "and he has been giving a piece of the diamond to the Beatles, [to] everyone he has been working with. He wants to retire, so the piece of the diamond is getting smaller, and he found a way to chip the diamond again and give me a piece. I felt very fortunate to spend some time with him."

Celine had never met Carole King before they teamed up at Martin's Air Studios in London for "The Reason," but was a longtime fan of King's, whose recorded work stems back to the late fifties. As a songwriter King has been placing tunes on the charts since the early sixties, with "Will You Still Love Me Tomorrow?" by the Shirelles, "Take Good Care of My Baby" by Bobby Vee, and the Drifters' "Up on the Roof," all written in collaboration with Gerry Goffin. Further hits followed for Aretha Franklin and the Monkees. In 1971 she stepped in front of the microphone once more, scoring a major hit with *Tapestry*, an album that spawned two chart toppers, "It's Too Late" and "So Far Away." *Tapestry* sold in excess of 10 million copies, establishing King as one of the premier songwriters of her generation. "The Reason" was just the latest song on King's already impressive résumé.

When King entered the studio she was relaxed, and greeted Celine with a casual, "Hey, girlfriend! How ya doin'." They jumped into one another's arms and started working right away. Celine noted King's generosity in the studio, the kind of respect one professional gives another. King was on cloud nine, saying it would be impossible for any songwriter not to want Celine Dion to sing her song.

The finished track of "The Reason," with King on background vocals, turned out just the way Martin had planned. "I get a big kick out of doing something I think is very worthwhile like this track with Celine," he said. "It was a high."

* * *

Years of hard work—endless touring, prolific recording, and shrewd marketing—had turned Celine into show-business royalty with a bank account to match her regal status. In 1997 she made her debut on the *Forbes* list of the highest-paid entertainers.

Topping the stellar list was movie machine Steven Spielberg, who earned an estimated $313 million in 1996–97. He had reigned over the *Forbes* list in 1994 and 1995, falling to the number-two position in 1996, just behind Oprah Winfrey. The success of *The Lost World*, the sequel to *Jurassic Park*, put him back on top in 1997.

Producer-director George Lucas came in second with earnings of $241 million; talk-show maven Oprah Winfrey fell to third place with a take of $201 million; fourth was author Michael Crichton, who brought in $102 million; rounding out the multimillionaires top five was the Beatles, who raked in $98 million, a full twenty-seven years after they had gone their separate ways.

Celine's income of $65 million placed her in the fifteenth position, wedged between writer John Grisham (#14) and rock-and-roll legend David Bowie (#16). Other moneymaking musicians in the top forty include the venerable Rolling Stones (#12 with $68 million), ex-Police bassist Sting (#20 with $57 million), country music's Garth Brooks (#21 with $55 million) who is tied with the King of Pop Michael Jackson also with earnings of $55 million, shock-rockers Kiss (#30 with $48 million), Miami Sound Machine's Gloria Estefan (#31 with $47 million), British singing sensations the Spice Girls (#32 with $47 million), hot music producer Babyface

(#33 with $44 million), and Irish rockers U2 (#38 with $40 million).

At age twenty-nine Celine Dion was now one of the highest-paid performers in the music business.

Celine admits to not knowing very much about classical music, although she recognizes that it takes a "big talent to do opera singing." One thing she does know about classical music is the name Luciano Pavarotti. They share the same vocal doctor, and one day several years ago met at the doctor's home. She was struck by his charisma and awed by his reputation.

Celine had wanted to work with Pavarotti since their chance meeting at the doctor's house, and the track "I Hate You Then I Love You" offered the perfect chance. Pavarotti was no stranger to pop music, having teamed up with Bryan Adams, Sting, Bono, and Dolores O'Riordan on record. It takes a special song to contain two huge voices—Pavarotti's booming vocals and Celine's five-octave range—and this tune had the height and breadth to allow both remarkable singers to work.

In the studio Celine was amazed at the power of Pavarotti's voice. She noted that when the opera singer sang next to her, she needed a microphone, but Luciano didn't. "[His voice] is so loud. . . . You vibrate being near [him]."

Because Let's Talk About Love was recorded in studios all over the world, Celine spent most of 1997 on the move. That gave her ample time between recording sessions to make public appearances. She took time out to appear at charity shows, as well as the Junos, the Grammys, and one other prestigious music awards show.

The World Music Awards are held each year in Monte Carlo, Monaco. Awards are granted using only one criterion—record sales. The event routinely attracts the world's biggest music stars, drawn by the dazzling ceremony. The 1997 edition was a particularly glitzy affair, given that Monaco's Princess Stephanie was the host and Prince Albert presided. Alanis Morisette and Oasis won in both the rock and alternative categories, while the Fugees took home an award for best-selling pop group. Lionel Richie and the Bee Gees were honored with "legend" statues. Celine was given an award for best-selling pop artist.

She was very busy, but took time away from her schedule to appear because the awards system appealed to her philanthropic side. Half the proceeds of the show go to the Princess Grace Foundation to aid young artists and the elderly, orphans, and underprivileged children. The rest goes to a hospital in Madagascar.

Celine has always been a big supporter of charity, selflessly giving her time to the Cystic Fibrosis Foundation ("I think it's the greatest cause," she says) among others. Artists of her stature are always being asked to lend their support to various charities, but because of scheduling conflicts, they aren't always able to appear at a fund-raising concert or dinner. Celine's commitment to helping others means that she tries to make herself available as much as possible.

One example of her humanitarian efforts benefited the Ottawa General Hospital and the Sisters of Charity.

"Our foundation wanted to do an event as our contribution to the 150th anniversary celebration of the Sisters," says Thom Nesbitt, acting executive director of the Sisters of Charity Health Service Foundation. "We wanted to do something that was appropriate and also something that would demonstrate what the Sisters are all about. In their own quiet, modest way, they reach out to people."

Celine committed to appearing at a fund-raising gala at the Ottawa Congress Center after a brief chat with Sister Diane Albert. The sister visited with her before a show at the National Arts Center to ask her to perform at the benefit. "It was like a one-minute interview just before her concert," said Sister Diane. The chat was brief, but Celine gladly agreed to the offer.

By lending her name to the concert, Celine raised a great deal of money to benefit the Ottawa General Hospital (tickets started at $150), but also increased the charity's profile. "Dion should draw young people's attention to the work of the Elisabeth Bruyère Health Center [contained within the Ottawa General Hospital], which is part of the Sisters of Charity Health Service," said Nesbitt. "The event [was] good for the Sisters," she added, "because their lifestyle does not usually allow them to attend such shows. Obviously [Celine] thought this was a good cause."

The strong sense of family values instilled in all the Dion children by her mother Thérèse compels Celine to use her station in life to benefit others. Good works aside, though, now it was time to get back to recording her new album.

* * *

The next tune on *Let's Talk About Love* was a song Celine almost turned down. Composer James Horner— known for his film scores for *Field of Dreams*, *The Rocketeer*, and *Braveheart*—sat at a piano and played "My Heart Will Go On" for René and Celine. "He couldn't sing it and he couldn't play every note of the song," said Celine, laughing at the memory.

Horner explained that he planned to use the song as the closing credit theme for a new James Cameron film titled *Titanic*. The film was notorious in Hollywood circles for its spiraling budget, then rumored to be approaching the $200 million mark—the most expensive film ever produced. Horner also explained that director Cameron didn't want any pop songs included on the film's score, but the composer felt *Titanic* needed something to sum up the character Rose's feelings for Jack at the film's end. In secret he commissioned lyricist Will Jennings to compose words to the movie's love theme. If Celine was willing to record the tune, they would have to do it on the sly.

Horner's less-than-inspiring rendition of the song notwithstanding, Celine liked "My Heart Will Go On" and admired the composer's belief in the tune. "René kind of stopped James Horner and said, 'You believe in the song so much, maybe Celine should do a demo,'" said Celine. "'You present the song to James Cameron whenever you want. And if he wants to go for it, we'll go back to the studio and we'll record it again.'"

In May 1997, according to Horner, the singer and "twelve to fifteen of Celine's closest Sony friends" reported to New York City's Hit Factory recording studio to make the demo. Celine was tense. She hadn't been in the studio for some time, and the secrecy surrounding this session was making her nervous. Breaking from her usual routine of drinking water before recording, she drank two cups of coffee instead. The combination of the caffeine and nerves influenced her performance.

"I couldn't control my voice," she says. "I was shaking and sweating; I could hear my knees." Ultimately, though, her physical and mental state served the song, forcing her to throw herself into the music.

Horner was pleased with the demo, but waited a month to play it for James Cameron. The composer didn't want to annoy Cameron with the pop song, as the director was under the gun from budget overruns and release-date delays. When at last he heard it, the director thought "My Heart Will Go On" was the perfect song to close his epic film.

"He said, 'I love it, Celine sings it great,' " said the singer. "And I didn't sing it again, so the demo is what people hear. We all felt as if it was a magic moment, and we didn't want to re-create it."

Before agreeing to allow the song to be used in *Titanic*, René arranged an early screening. He had already turned down one movie soundtrack offer that summer. He declined use of one of Celine's songs in *Con Air* and wanted to make sure *Titanic* was "good enough" before lending her name to the credits.

Titanic stole Celine's heart. "They did an amazing job with the tragedy of the *Titanic*," she said after the screening. She was taken with the love story between

Jack and Rose, a love that bloomed amid the death and destruction of the huge ship slowly sinking to the murky depths. "They came up with the love story that happens on the boat, while people are waiting for death. . . . The whole thing is just heartbreaking."

A deal was worked to include the demo of "My Heart Will Go On" on the soundtrack, and a slickly rerecorded Celtic-tinted version of it on *Let's Talk About Love*. Celine loved the song, but had no idea how popular it would become.

"Who knew what impact it would have on people?" she says. "You have a very strong love story to make people cry, and to make them want to hear the song and see the film three, four, and five times. It's a magic moment, and I'm glad they thought about me. I'm very proud that we said yes to do it."

Celine says there are two people she looks up to. One is a woman she calls her idol—her mother, Thérèse. On the show-business side of life, her idol is Barbra Streisand.

By any standard, Streisand is an entertainment legend. From her first professional acting job at age fifteen to her solo recording debut at twenty-one, she showed a single-minded determination to be a star. Like Celine, Streisand is a perfectionist, who throughout her career has exerted control over every aspect of the projects she has been involved in. After winning an Academy Award in 1968 for her role as Fanny Brice in *Funny Girl*, Streisand turned to producing, directing, and starring in films. As a multitalented performer, there seemed to be no discipline she couldn't master. She was a musical-theater star on Broadway. Her albums sold in the millions, and film after film topped the box office. Career highs include the films *What's Up, Doc?* (1972), *The Way We Were* (1973), *A Star Is Born* (1978), and *Yentl* (1983), and hit songs with Neil Diamond ("You Don't Bring Me Flowers") and Donna Summers ("Enough Is Enough"). It is Streisand's voice that is a true marvel. Years of Broadway training have given her a strong sweet instrument, tempered with a sense of the dramatic that turns whatever song she sings into an aria. As the only female artist ever to top the album charts in four consecutive decades, Streisand's reputation as a singer is unparalleled.

A duet between Celine and Streisand had been in the works for some time. David Foster (who produced most of Celine's big hits, and also helmed Streisand's 1993 *Back to Broadway*) says he always wanted to bring the two singers together. Celine and Streisand became friendly after the Academy Awards fiasco, when the press reported that Streisand had snubbed Celine. They started talking after Streisand's congratulatory note to Celine, thanking her for doing such a beautiful version of "I Finally Found Someone" and suggesting that they "make one together."

Foster was brought in as a liaison between the two superstars. A deal was quickly worked out. Foster, along with his wife Linda Thompson and producer Walter Afanasieff, wrote "Tell Him," an inspirational power ballad that would showcase both singers. The songwriters framed the tune as a conversation between a younger woman asking an elder for some love advice. To be fair to both performers, "Tell Him" would appear on both Celine's *Let's Talk About Love* and Streisand's *Higher Ground*.

The top-secret session, which the press billed as "Diva Duel of the Decade" was a musical moment Celine will never forget. She says meeting Streisand was a thrill, but singing with her was the best musical experience she had ever had in her life. She adds that she doesn't think anything will ever top that meeting. "Hearing her voice so close to me, I felt complete. I was so close to her breath, her emotion, her soul. I was finally singing with somebody I have been admiring all my life.

"When I got the tape in the studio, it was time to put my voice on it. I put [on] the tape, [pressed] play, and I sat back and I heard her voice, and I was like an animal in a cage because I was like, 'Open the mike, I'm ready to go.' "

While the session's official photographer, Herb Ritts, documented the historic recording, Celine and Streisand did their best to make the studio atmosphere joyful. Ritts's photographs show two professionals clearly enraptured with one another. They hold hands. They hug. Ear-to-ear smiles beam from their faces. "She's the best in the world," said Celine. "I love her."

With so much star power on one song, obviously "Tell Him" was planned as the commercial centerpiece of *Let's Talk About Love*. At the playback in the studio, everyone was electrified. Celine and Streisand's voices are pitted against a thunderous background, soaring and swooping, conjuring up one of the most dramatic pop singles in years. Foster wasn't surprised at the chemistry between the dueling divas. He says he knew what the song would sound like, what the singers would do with it, from the moment he wrote it. "Honestly," he says, "when I heard that finished mix, it was like that's what I envisioned."

Demand was so strong for the powerhouse Streisand-Celine duet that Sony records delivered "Tell Him" via satellite to radio stations across North America in early October, a full month before *Let's Talk About Love* was scheduled to hit the stores.

Subsequent to that historic recording session, Celine and Streisand have stayed in touch. The first time they had dinner together at Streisand's home, Celine was still in awe. Describing the dinner, she sounds more like a groupie than a peer. "She was eating her food like a normal person," Celine gushed, recalling the meal. She stopped herself from staring at Streisand, telling herself, "Snap out of it because she's going to ask you to leave."

Since then they have kept in touch, and Celine says she is still a huge fan.

Tears flowed at the next recording session. Maurice, Robin, and Barry Gibb, better known as the Bee Gees, were inspired by Celine to write a tune called "Immortality." Barry Gibb describes Celine as the best female pop singer working today, so it was a dream come true to have her record one of his songs.

The three brothers have had a long and distinguished career. Their first chart entry came with an Australian single called "Spicks and Specks" in 1966. For the rest of the sixties they seemed unstoppable. A string of Beatles-like singles rocketed up the charts, one after the other, starting with "New York Mining Disaster, 1941," followed by "To Love Somebody," "Massachusetts," and "Words." Then, in the early seventies, the hits dried up and the group was reduced to playing cabaret shows. A low point came at the Yorkshire Variety Club performance in front of an abusive audience more interested in drinking than listening to love songs. Atlantic Records' refusal to release their LP *A Kick in the Head Is Worth Eight in the Pants* seemed to sound the band's death knell. Then came "Jive Talkin'." It was a Goliath hit in May 1975, reestablishing them on the charts and leading to a string of singles that turned them into the biggest act of the 1970s. They continue to flourish as performers and songwriters.

"Immortality" is a special song. Maurice Gibb says it is about every performer's dream—to have their work remembered after they are gone. Celine understood the deeper meaning of the song immediately and was eager to work with the Bee Gees. She says she had danced to their music for years, but more than that, she was proud for the people of Quebec that the Bee Gees had embraced her, and written a song for her. "I feel very proud that they have chosen me to do that," she says.

The night of the session was a revelation for Maurice, Robin, and Barry. They knew of Celine's work but had never heard her sing "Immortality." After some rehearsal they entered the studio to record the vocals. With the Bee Gees supplying their trademark smooth harmony, Celine laid down a seamless vocal, so full of emotion that it brought tears to the songwriters' eyes. "I've admired them for so long," said Celine, "and to have them react like that . . . I believe people who cry, they're being blessed."

"The first time we heard ['Immortality'] it was very

teary," says Barry. He says that Celine has one of the most beautiful voices in the world, and when he sat there listening to her sing his material, it hit him on an emotional level. All three brothers agreed that Celine's "Immortality" session was a magic moment, a high point in their recording careers. None of them will ever forget that night.

Celine loves the song and plans to use it to close her live shows. She explains that "Immortality" is the perfect song to sing as an encore, after she has been onstage for two hours and has given the audience everything. "I feel like coming back onstage, sitting on the edge and [starting] the song, and saying. 'This is who I am, this is all I know.' "

Let's Talk About Love gave Celine a chance to broaden her musical horizons. Breaking up the ballad-heavy playlist of the album is a reggae-influenced dance-hall number called "Treat Her Like a Lady"—Celine's only cowrite on the disc; she wrote it with dance-hall star Diana King, Andy Marvel, and Billy Mann. Taylor Dayne producer Ric Wake was brought in to guide Celine through the difficult rap lyrics. Indeed, "Lady" is a radical departure for the singer, as it features the first-ever DJ scratching and rap on any of her records. Showing a willingness to experiment, she also tackled the Spanish lyrics of "Amar Haciendo el Amor."

"Everyone should make an effort to learn another language," said Celine when she began Spanish lessons. Learning new languages satisfied her desire to educate herself, but also opened up new markets in her plan for world domination. "I would like to have a career like Julio Iglesias. He can sing in any language, and is known everywhere in the world."

The fifteen cuts on *Let's Talk About Love* show Celine working at peak form. Over the course of her English-language albums she had developed into a fine song stylist, capable of working in many genres, throwing heart and soul into every song. Backed by the best producers, singers, and musicians working today, *Let's Talk About Love* sparkles, showcasing Celine's remarkable range. She describes the record as her best work, "the album of my life."

Critics agreed. Reviewing the album, *Billboard* saved its heaviest praise for the diva duet. "Talk about an event," the magazine gushed. "Two of pop music's best voices are united on a grand, wonderfully over-the-top ballad that will melt the heart of even the most jaded listener. No one will be able to resist the electricity resulting from the blend of their voices."

As 1997 turned into 1998, many commentators in the press tried to sum up the impact that Canadian women had made on the world of show business. Nobody did it better than Rex Murphy, speaking on the New Year's Eve edition of CBC-TV's *National Magazine*. "Celine Dion has now sung with Barbra Streisand, which in the high-toned world of pop 'diva-dom' must be seen as an act of apostolic succession. Alanis Morisette is a headline draw from Morocco to Moosejaw. Shania Twain, whose belly button is an entire solar system unto itself, has done more for country and western than heartbreak and whiskey combined."

Those three women were Canada's leading exports, but with the help of a movie love theme, Celine would soon eclipse them all.

CHAPTER FIFTEEN

——————————◆

Titanic Sales

Let's talk about numbers.

Released in Canada on November 18, 1997, *Let's Talk About Love* sold a staggering 230,212 copies in its first week of release. That broke the record previously held by the Florida all-boy group Backstreet Boys, who moved 67,043 records in one week earlier that same year. Sales in excess of 200,000 gave *Let's Talk About Love* the biggest opening-week sales ever in Canadian history.

"One out of every one hundred Canadians purchased *Let's Talk About Love* in its first week," said Doug Spence, director of Canadian operations for Soundscan, a company that monitors record sales. "That's a phenomenal statistic." Sixty percent of those sales were in Celine's home province of Quebec.

In the all-important American market the album debuted at number two on *Billboard*'s Top 200 album chart, just behind Metallica's *Re-Load*. Outside North America, the album debuted at number one in Britain, Australia, France, Holland, and South Africa. In fact, the demand for *Let's Talk About Love* was so strong, Sony shipped one million albums to the Canadian stores in the first week—a record-industry milestone. "It's the largest shipping album in the history of the Canadian music industry," said Don Oates, Sony's senior sales vice president.

Record stores were ready for the Celine onslaught, which most retailers agreed kicked off the 1997 Christmas season. "It's a humongous, huge, gigantic event," said Denis Germain, marketing manager for HMV in Montreal. Germain adds that no record since the Beatles' 1995 *Anthology* has generated as much excitement. The demand for *Let's Talk About Love* was so great, in fact, that Sony had to cut down on orders from the stores. Germain wouldn't say how many copies of the disc HMV ordered, but noted that even with Sony cutting their order by 50 percent, they could still set a sales record if they sold out their entire stock. "I've been in this business for fifteen years and this is the biggest I've seen," raved Marc Melanson, pop-music buyer for Archambault Musique stores.

In Ottawa copies of the album were snapped up as soon as employees could unpack them from the shipping cases. "It's been craziness around here. . . . It's good to see," said Brant Beckta of the Rideau Centre branch of HMV. Many stores opened several hours early on November 18 to accommodate the crush of record buyers lining up to be the first to own *Let's Talk About Love*. Store owners say Celine was good for business all around. "In some ways, this sort of thing renews confidence in the recording business," says Beckta. "A hot record gets people hot about all kinds of records. . . . It just spills over." In other words, customers coming into the store to buy Celine's record are likely to pick up any of the dozens of new releases by other artists.

"It's not just Celine, of course, but she starts it all," said one retailer. "She's brought the excitement back. It should be a good Christmas."

Sony tried to meet demand, keeping pressing plants open night and day for three weeks, shipping the CDs out to the stores as soon as they were manufactured. "She's brought hype and excitement back to the stores," said Germain.

The album was flying out of the stores. From Australia to the United Kingdom it was top of the pops. Celine's career was at an all-time high. Then, at a four-hour press conference, the superstar dropped a bombshell on her fans: she was ready to retire.

Two hundred reporters from around North America had assembled in east-end Montreal's CFTM television studio to watch a video presentation on the making of the album. Later Celine would take questions. When she was discussing her plans for the future, her comments surprised everyone in the room. Hinting that she might take a long break, she seemed happy and comfortable with the decision.

"If this is my last album, if this is over, I feel very complete. I've done everything I've always wanted. If this has to be over after this one, I can leave without regretting anything."

Reporters pressed her to clarify. Does this mean she's retiring from music? "Maybe. You never know. *[Let's Talk About Love]* is the best I can give," she told reporters. "Maybe it's better not to do another. I don't want to bore people with my music. I want to stop for a little while, do something else, and come back again."

Without getting too specific, Celine suggested she was ready for a career change. "I want to do some acting, to do some movies." Both she and René were coy when questioned about what kind of movies Celine would appear in. René would do no more than confirm that they are considering two acting projects but refused further detail.

At least one of her new fans didn't want her to stop singing. When Sir George Martin heard the news he was heartsick. He emphatically urged Celine not to retire, saying that she has much in front of her. He added that the world would "love to have her do more."

No one could have foreseen the impact *Titanic* would have on moviegoers. Just six weeks before the film opened in theaters, high-ranking executives at Paramount and Twentieth Century-Fox privately admitted doubts that the film would ever stray into the black. Their fears, however, were unfounded. *Titanic* stayed at the number-one box-office position for an unprecedented fifteen weeks, raking in over $1 billion. Released in December 1997, the movie quickly transcended mere Hollywood commerce, becoming a cultural phenomenon. The *Titanic* juggernaut was impossible to escape. Some examples:

A Swiss–U.S. group announced it would build a $500 million, full-size replica of the luxury liner, scheduled to cross the Atlantic on the tragedy's ninetieth anniversary in April 2002. Tickets for the voyage will cost $10,000 to $100,000. "We thought now would be the right moment, because the whole world is keen on *Titanic*," said Annette Voelcker, a spokesman for the project's chief shareholder. "It will have modern equipment to detect icebergs," she added.

A coffee-table book on the making of the film, *James Cameron's Titanic,* topped the *New York Times* best-seller list. A cookbook with recipes from the *Titanic*'s kitchen did brisk business, while *A Night to Remember*, a fifty-year-old book on the disaster, was reissued, selling 500,000 copies. No fewer than one dozen television specials were commissioned on the making of the film and the fateful night when the ship went down.

No detail was too small to debate. Internet chat rooms burned with *Titanic* lore. Here are some random examples: A Pomeranian was one of only three dogs known to have survived the wreck; the average person would stay alive for only thirty seconds in freezing water; a charcoal drawing could survive eighty-five years underwater, as long as it was inside a leatherbound portfolio; and the most expensive pieces of jewelry on board the ship were two strings of pearls belonging to Philadelphian Eleanor Widener, valued at $1 million.

The world was gripped with *Titanic* fever, and Celine was right in the middle of it all. Her contribution to the *Titanic* soundtrack, the haunting ballad "My Heart Will Go On," struck a chord with listeners, entering *Billboard*'s singles chart at number one. Teenage girls began holding crying parties, sobbing in groups while they listened to the *Titanic* soundtrack. "It's a little crazy," Celine says. "Are they doing it for therapy or something? I hope they find something positive. Crying can be good therapy."

Once again Celine shattered a music-industry record. In the week ending January 27, 1998, *Billboard* magazine's Broadcast Data Systems reported that "My Heart Will Go On" broke the all-time record for largest radio audience. According to BDS, a company that monitors airplay of radio stations reaching 98 percent of the U.S. population, the single was heard by more than 105.6 million listeners in a seven-day span. That beat the previous record holder, Donna Lewis's "I Love You Always Forever" by 5 million listeners.

Meanwhile the *Titanic* soundtrack rocketed up the charts. Unlike the real *Titanic*, this record proved unsinkable. Record buyers reacted so positively to the soundtrack because unlike most pop compilations, which contain songs not actually heard in the film, *Titanic*'s score actually appears in the movie, acting as an emotional souvenir. Sony Classics, the record company responsible for the soundtrack album, reported that orders in excess of 8 million copies led the Sony Music family to its biggest February in history. The album went to number one in fourteen countries (from France to Malaysia) and broke a *Billboard* record, selling 500,000 copies for six consecutive weeks in the U.S. It easily surpassed *Chariots of Fire* as the best-selling instrumental film score of all time. Sales were so brisk that one report claimed that Sony Classics will gross more from sales of the *Titanic* soundtrack than the label's entire catalog did in 1997. Typically sales of most instrumental movie scores are lucky to break five digits.

Entertainment Weekly touted Celine as "the voice that launched fifteen million albums."

The big loser in the *Titanic* soundtrack sweepstakes appears to be Polygram Records. They had released Horner's score for *Braveheart* in 1995, but took a pass on the *Titanic*. Horner offered them the album (he says he "begged them to do it") before Celine became involved with the project. The feeling at the Polygram office was that James Cameron, best known for mega action flicks like *The Terminator* and *The Abyss*, wouldn't be able to sustain a love story. Also they felt the asking price, rumored to be in excess of $1 million, was too steep. Executive vice president for Polygram Classics and Jazz admits to making a huge error in turning Horner away. "Was it in retrospect wrong?" she asks rhetorically. "Absolutely."

Composer James Horner received an up-front scoring fee of $800,000 for his soundtrack work, but that is just the tip of the iceberg. He also receives royalty points on the instrumental soundtrack and shares publishing and songwriting fees for "My Heart Will Go On." The show-business bible *Variety* noted that Horner will take home $1.20 for each album sold—a rate usually reserved for such superstar acts as Madonna and Michael Jackson.

Let's Talk About Love, buoyed by "My Heart Will Go On," became Celine's fastest-selling record ever, doubling the sales pace set by her previous album *Falling into You*.

While Celine was in Europe on a promotional tour, she met an unlikely fan. She was in Germany, performing on a talk show, when she bumped into Madonna, also appearing on the show. The two superstars performed their hit singles and spoke with the host.

"If only my father knew that I was sitting on the same couch as Celine Dion, he would die," said Madonna. Later, backstage, she told a reporter, "I think [Celine] is beautifully elegant and very, very nice. We congratulated each other, and I told her my father plays her CDs all the time."

Madonna wasn't the only pop diva to laud Celine. Liza Minnelli, daughter of the legendary singer/actress Judy Garland and film director Vincent Minnelli, sang her praises in an interview. "Celine, I think, is divine and she sings just like I do," said Minnelli. "Do you know what I mean? We're belters."

The hype was so thick you could have cut it with a knife. STREISAND TO TEAM WITH DION the headlines screamed. It had been announced that Celine and Streisand would re-create their powerful "Tell Him" duet live onstage at the Grammys. This set the music press on fire. Streisand was notoriously stage-shy, and after the Academy Awards fracas it appeared as though she was eating humble pie.

The pairing of the divas was planned as the show's climax. "I think it's going to be spectacular," said veteran Grammy producer Ken Ehrilch. "We have a relationship with both Celine and Barbra that goes back a long time. Barbra's been on the show several times. Celine has been on the show at least a couple of times. In all fairness, I really have to credit René, who really felt that this would be terrific to do on the Grammys, with kind of helping it along. I don't want to say convincing Barbra, 'cause it wasn't that, it was just making sure everything was right for us to put it together."

The focus of the 1998 Grammys was on live performance. Earlier shows had strayed from the tried-and-true formula of presenting the best in music, becoming speech-heavy. With the 1998 ceremony Ehrilch hoped to bring back the excitement of performance to the show. "The kind of show we do, I've often likened it to the Rose Parade," he said, "where the floats just move past you and then move elsewhere—the floats being the performances." In addition to the Streisand-Celine matchup, Ehrlich booked Lillith Fair founder Sarah McLachlan, Paula "Where Have All the Cowboys Gone?" Cole, and Shawn Colvin, rock legend Bob Dylan, the reunited Fleetwood Mac, Aretha Franklin and the Blues Brothers, Babyface and Stevie Wonder, teen heartthrobs Hanson, rapper-turned-actor Will Smith, teenage country-music sensation LeAnn Rimes, and Vince Gill. That's quite a lineup.

"Our mandate with this show," said Ehrlich, "even though it's about recorded music, is to create the most exciting live performances onstage, knowing that if we do it right there, it will translate to the viewer as something special and unique and different."

Celine was as excited about the planned duet as anybody. She told Oprah that the details had all been worked out—even what they would wear. No clashing colors. "It's all set," she said. "We're going to blend."

Then disaster struck. Just one week after Celine had gushed to Oprah about the Grammy appearance, Barbra issued a statement via her public-relations company. Just two days before the broadcast she had to cancel a Grammy rehearsal due to illness. "Her doctor is not yet able to determine if the illness will prevent her performance at the awards ceremony," said Streisand's spokesman Dick Guttman. She had a fever and the flu and was being treated with antibiotics.

The day of the show Guttman Associates released another announcement saying Streisand had the flu and fever and was "disappointed that she would not be able to sing with Celine Dion at the Grammy Awards." Instead, Celine would perform a solo version of "My Heart Will Go On."

Immediately the press jumped on the story, insinuating that Barbra might not actually have been sick. One tabloid dubbed her illness "the diplomatic flu," which had been incubating for five months since the pair collaborated on the "Tell Him" video shoot. The story implied that Streisand was nervous about appearing with Celine, whose "star is outshining hers."

The *New York Post* concurred, saying it wasn't the flu that prevented Streisand from making the show. The newspaper quoted friends and close associates as saying that because she hates performing live, she was worried she wouldn't have enough time to rehearse and feared that "Tell Him" wouldn't win an award. "She could have pushed herself," said one insider, "but when push came to shove, she didn't really want to do it."

Carole Glines, writing in *The Globe*, summed up the public-relations nightmare, quoting an insider: "Barbra could've shown her stuff. Instead Celine has emerged as the heroine." Streisand's spokesman maintained that the singer was simply too ill to perform.

Celine couldn't have been pleased when late-night comedy show *Saturday Night Live* lampooned her. In a mean-spirited skit titled "The Celine Dion Show," *SNL* cast member Ana Gasteyer gave a devastating performance as Celine, poking fun at her slender frame, marriage to René, and dramatic singing style. As Celine,

Gasteyer railed at her other guests, Mariah Carey (played by Cheri Oteri), and Erykah Badu (played by Tim Meadows). "I'm so sorry, Mariah, but don't be jealous that I have the best voice in the world," said Gasteyer. "Once, I didn't have everything. I was a homely, twelve-year-old girl, French-Canadian, with acorn breasts, who had to take her forty-five-year-old manager to her first dance." To "Badu" she said, "If I wasn't such a nice person, I'd think I was a show-off."

A debate raged on the *Saturday Night Live* Web site the following day on the appropriateness of the skit. "She is not known as a prima donna, blowhard, or anything else that would lend itself to comedy," wrote one outraged fan. Another fan voiced his displeasure, sending a message to the skit's writers. "Obviously you don't live in Canada or read the tabloids," he wrote.

Celine had no comment.

Once again, in 1998, the Academy came calling. Like everyone else in the world, the Academy couldn't seem to get enough of the *Titanic*. The most expensive movie ever made raked in an amazing fourteen nominations— everything from Best Picture and Best Director to Best Costumes and, of course, Best Original Song for "My Heart Will Go On." Only once before had a film been honored with so many nominations. Not since 1950's *All About Eve* had one film so dominated the Oscars.

During the ceremony host Billy Crystal couldn't resist wisecracking at the expense of the epic film. During the show's opening song he serenaded the *Titanic*'s crew to the tune of *Gilligan's Island*. Remarking on *Titanic*'s Oscar-nominated clothing designs, he said, "And the best thing is that those costumes are drip-dry." Following a brief film clip showing the ship sinking into the water, he joked. "That clip cost $15 million. The only thing I saw retaining water faster than that was my aunt Stella after eating shellfish."

As the three-hour-forty-seven-minute ceremony unfolded, it was clear that it was *Titanic*'s night. Statue after statue went to the film—Visual Effects, Film Editing, Costume, Original Dramatic Score, Sound Effects Editing, Sound, Cinematography, Art Direction, Director, and, the most coveted, Best Picture. Celine had a hand in the film's other win—Best Original Song.

She was up against tunes from some of the year's most successful movies—*Hercules* ("Go the Distance"), *Anastasia* ("Journey to the Past"), *Con Air* ("How Do I Live?"), and *Good Will Hunting* ("Miss Misery"). None of the songs equaled the power and passion (and sales) of "My Heart Will Go On," and most industry insiders agreed that Horner and Celine would walk away with an Oscar.

Wearing a high-necked, floor-length blue Halston gown, Celine gave a sensitive reading of "My Heart Will Go On" accompanied by the Academy orchestra. Around her neck was a re-creation of Le Coeur de la Mer (the Heart of the Ocean), the spectacular diamond-and-sapphire necklace that is at the heart of *Titanic*'s love story. Designed by Asprey of London, the 170-carat sapphire was a stunning addition to her couture dress. "It's like Versailles," said Celine, comparing the necklace with the French palace. "It's a work of art." She added that the piece was "a thrill to wear."

The necklace was on loan from Asprey, having been

auctioned to an anonymous bidder for $2.2 million two nights before the ceremony. To Celine's surprise, it was revealed several days after the show that the anonymous bidder was René, who purchased the bauble as a birthday gift for his wife.

In total, *Titanic* captured eleven Academy Awards, tying the record for all-time wins. The Academy denied the epic only three awards, for Best Makeup (which deservedly went to *Men in Black*), Best Supporting Actress (Gloria Stuart lost to Kim Basinger for *L.A. Confidential*), and Best Actress (Helen Hunt for *As Good As It Gets*, instead of Kate Winslet). When a reporter asked director James Cameron if he was upset that *Titanic* didn't break *Ben Hur*'s record for all-time wins, he replied jokingly, "I'm so pissed off about that."

After the show Celine rubbed elbows with Hollywood's biggest stars at the Governor's Ball, the official Oscar party held next door to the Shrine Auditorium. While she and René dined on chef Wolfgang Puck's marinated lobster salad, avocado sushi, smoked salmon on Oscar-shaped matzos, and chicken breasts with wild mushroom risotto, even she was starstruck.

The 1,650 revelers were ready to let loose after the almost four-hour-long show. One guest, Alec Baldwin, had some advice for first-time Oscar winner Matt Damon. "Stay off the drugs, stay off the booze," said Baldwin, "and we're all pulling for you." Damon, pumped up after his big win for Best Screenplay for *Good Will Hunting*, was taken aback. "Tonight?" he protested. "The booze?"

Celine mingled with the glitterati, chatting with Robin Williams, Billy Crystal, Ben Affleck, and a host of others, all the while marveling at how a girl from a tiny town in Quebec could have reached the apex of show-business glamour.

When the television ratings came in, *Titanic* proved to be a bonanza for the Oscars. Variety reported the highest rating in fifteen years for an Academy Awards broadcast. The magazine credited the appeal of *Titanic* with the boost in viewership.

The Oscars' household rating in the United States jumped 27 percent over 1997's show, according to Nielsen Media Research. The broadcast reached 34.9 percent of homes in the U.S., but more impressive than that was the increase in younger demographics. The two-to-eleven age-group rating showed a 98 percent jump compared with 1997. The research agency also noted an increase in teen and young-adult viewership—71 percent and 72 percent respectively.

"Even though you think of this as an adult viewing event, if you give them youthful stars, kids will watch in large numbers," said Dene Gallas, senior vice president of Grey Media analysis. She goes on to credit *Titanic* stars Kate Winslet and Leonardo DiCaprio for the leap in youthful attention.

It's late March 1998. The occasion is an intimate reception for seventy journalists at Celine and René's palatial offices in suburban Montreal. They have gathered among the award-lined walls to find out who will be the opening act for Celine's upcoming world tour. The real event, however, as newspaper man Ray Conlogue put it, is "the offices themselves, a veritable felled forest of exotic wood panelling and the whispered possibility that Dion herself might appear."

The adornments of the offices are truly spectacular, fit for a queen. Herringbone floors stretch out through the many halls and chambers. Complementing the handsome wooden floors are triangular harlequin designs on the walls in mahogany and rosewood. Overstuffed leather couches invite guests to relax while René works behind his vast Louis XIV–style desk. Celine designed the digs herself. "She had a stack of European design magazines, and she did exactly what she wanted," said René.

It is a testament to Celine's incredible star power that a seasoned arts reporter like Conlogue would be aflutter at the possibility of meeting her. He reports that after a short press conference with Quebec impressionist and warm-up act André-Philippe Gagnon, "a new gravitational force [entered] the room." Celine had arrived. She made a few jokes with the press about having trouble getting past security at her own office. "I'm on the telephone at security downstairs," she said, laughing, "and I say, 'Hello, it's Celine,' and the people up here say, 'Yeah, right.' "

After posing for a several photos, she's off as quickly as she arrived. Conlogue continues his story, noting that Gagnon had the unenviable task of "re-focusing the shattered attention of the media, a foretaste of the tour to come."

The tour, which will take Celine and Gagnon around the world, was a sellout as soon as it was announced. In many cities tickets sold out in a matter of minutes. Just another example of the popularity of Queen Celine.

By the spring of 1998 Celine Dion had gathered every award that the music business has to offer. It was fitting, then, that her country and home province would see it as appropriate to bestow their highest honors on her.

On the eve of her thirtieth birthday, the governments of Canada and Quebec engaged in a tug-of-war as to who would claim her as their own. Canadian Governor-General Romeo LeBlanc announced that Celine would be appointed an officer of the Order of Canada in a ceremony in Ottawa on Friday, May 1. Order of Canada recipients are generally announced in batches in January and July; individual awards are very rare.

Mr. LeBlanc's announcement may have come in response to Quebec Premier Lucien Bouchard's statement that Celine would receive a comparable honor, the National Order of Quebec, on Thursday, April 30.

Pamela Miller, a spokeswoman for the governor-general, conceded that the situation was atypical. She denied that the announcement was made in answer to Bouchard's statement. "I guess the timing happened to coincide," she said. "Her nomination was accepted and recommended in January, but it was too late to be included in the January press release and would have been included in July, but because she was able to accept it in May, we announced it today."

René quickly quashed any rumors of political posturing. At a press conference he scolded the press for blowing this out of proportion. "There is no conflict between the two [awards]," he said. "It's normal that she receive this kind of honor. The only people who ask questions about it are journalists who love controversy."

Celine saw the dual awards as a way of declaring allegiance to both Canada and Quebec. Years before, in 1992, she made a rare political declaration, one that caused a storm of controversy in Quebec. The province was on the verge of a vote to decide whether to become a sovereign nation—that is, to separate from Canada and form a distinct country with its own cultural identity. At a press conference in Seville, Spain, she said she found the idea of Quebec separating from Canada "dreadful." Adding that she was "against all forms of separation, of course," she mentioned Switzerland as an example of a country where "there are three cultures that live in harmony. Canada should definitely stay together," she said.

Her comments drew the ire of columnists, making front-page news in Quebec. For the first time Quebeckers were upset with her. One radio station threatened to stop playing her music, and she was booed at her next Montreal appearance.

Celine was traumatized by the reaction in her home province and, fearing she would lose her audience, quickly tried to smooth things over. "Some people were left with the impression that I spoke up in defense of Canada," she countered, "which isn't the case at all. I don't speak for Canada. I even refused to do a 125th anniversary-of-confederation commercial because I didn't want to be used. I'm *québecoise* and proud to be called *québecoise*, whether Quebec is separate or not."

She declined, however, to flip-flop on her remarks regarding separatism. "It's true, I am not a separatist. I'm convinced that, for the moment, we have nothing to gain from separation. If I had my way there would be no borders anywhere in the world. But I am for Quebec and I am for a better world. I stand for the mutual respect of our two cultures." Thus endeth Celine's political career.

Writer Jean Beaunoyer says Celine reflects the "ambiguity of Quebec nationalism. It's the classic ... line about wanting an independent Quebec in a united Canada."

The day of the ceremony in Quebec, Premier Lucien Bouchard pinned the Order of Quebec to Celine's lapel, declaring, "Here and around the world, you are the best-known Quebecker ... You are therefore our greatest ambassador."

At the postceremony press conference, a spokesperson made it clear that Celine would stay clear of any controversial topics. "Mrs. Dion won't get involved in politics. She did that once and decided afterward that in the future she'll concentrate on doing her job—and politics isn't part of it."

The following day Celine flew to the capital of Canada, Ottawa, to receive the Order of Canada—an honor reserved for Canadians recognized for "national achievement and merit of the highest degree, especially service to Canada or humanity at large." She was honored for her charity work with the Canadian CF Foundation and other volunteer work. "Your talent, your discipline, and your dynamism have inspired young artists throughout the world," said Governor-General Romeo LeBlanc as he presented the award. "You have put your heart not only into your music, but also into your volunteer efforts."

Speaking to the press afterward, Celine denied that Quebec and Canada were engaged in a political tug-of-war to declare her as their own. "To me, what happened yesterday and what happened today have nothing to do with politics," she said. "Of course I'm from Quebec.

I'm from this little town called Charlemagne. But when people ask me everywhere if I'm a Quebecker or I'm a Canadian, I [say I] am both and very proud of it."

She closed out the press meet-and-greet by saying she has never striven for awards. "I have not been in show business to receive trophies and awards . . . but if they want to give it to me, with pleasure I will take them."

AFTERWORD

―――――◇

Dion and On and On

ONE CAN ONLY guess where Celine Dion will go from here. She is at the acme of the music business and just thirty years old.

Interview hyperbole notwithstanding, it seems unlikely that she will retire anytime soon. In a recent *People* magazine poll, one thousand readers (randomly selected and contacted by phone; median age 38.5 and 68 percent female) rated Celine as their favorite singer by a staggering margin; 17.2 percent of readers voted for her, handily beating out all the other competition. (Mariah Carey and Whitney Houston tied for second with 5.3 percent, while Barbra Streisand and Madonna scored 4.3 percent in fourth place.)

That kind of visible love and support from her fans will certainly be an irresistible draw to get her back into the studio. In fact, as we go to press, plans are in the works for a Christmas album to be released in the fall of 1998. The as-yet-untitled album will be recorded in English, in New York and Los Angeles. It isn't Celine's first attempt at Christmas music. In 1981 she released the French-language *Celine chante Noël*. More recently she has recorded "A Christmas Song" for a David Foster variety TV special, and "Petit Papa Noël" with the Chipmunks on *A Very Merry Chipmunk Christmas*.

Details about the new album are being kept under wraps. "It's going to be a blend of traditional Christmas and a few new songs," said a Sony spokesman. "I'd rather not give away the tunes at this stage only because we haven't decided on them yet. It involves certain producers and certain writers. We still haven't even totally involved everyone on our side."

Celine will also pop up on a kids' album. She has joined Elmo and Big Bird to commemorate the thirtieth anniversary of *Sesame Street*. Celebrations include a TV special, a soundtrack, and a video called *Elmopalooza*. The soundtrack features a bonus track by Celine.

Denise Donlan, director of music programming at Canada's twenty-four-hour-video station Much Music, has watched Celine mature, and feels she can do anything she puts her mind to. "If she puts her single-minded determination to anything else, I think she'd succeed. I would suggest possibly other styles of music. She may want to try different areas and go for something a bit more classical. I think she could share a stage with the opera greats. And she's so young. She could have three or four careers."

Doing good for others is one of the responsibilities that comes with the rarefied status Celine has achieved. She has more than fulfilled that obligation through her work with cystic fibrosis—work that will certainly continue—and no doubt will add to her charitable work. Recently she loaned her name to a Toronto-based effort to raise $1 million to help feed starving North Koreans. She did a series of radio and television public announcements to raise awareness of the situation in North Korea, where people have been dying of starvation because of many years of crop failure. Celine donated her time to make the announcements that were aired in Toronto and Quebec, and nationally in Canada on CBC-TV. No matter what twists and turns her life and career may take, it is certain that her commitment to helping others will continue.

Now that she has reached the pinnacle of musical success, other show-business avenues are open to her. Perhaps she will venture into films, as fellow divas Whitney Houston, Madonna, and Barbra Streisand have done.

There is an old showbiz proverb that says, "All actors want to sing, and all singers want to act." While there are many cases where singers should have remained singers and not tried their hand at acting, Celine has already proved she has what it takes. Her dramatic performance in *Des Fleurs sur la Neige* was well received, and now that she is fluent in English, making the leap to Hollywood would seem a natural. Lately rumors have been circulating on the Internet that Celine might star in a bio-pic on the life of fabled French singer Edith Piaf.

On a more personal note Celine still talks of wanting to start a family with René.

She has also expressed a desire to slow down the pace of her life. She told a television reporter that she craves a normal life with her husband. She wants to do the things that normal married couples do—go for a picnic, lounge around the house in a bathrobe, go to a movie—

and spend more time with René. She is concerned that her husband is not getting any younger and worries that if they spend the next few years working—just trying to make more money—they will never have the chance to enjoy each other, as man and wife should.

Even though Celine would like more from their marriage, she is still as happy as the day of the wedding. Recently she told a reporter that she is very much in love, adding that René completes her, makes her feel whole. Their union seems as stable and successful as Celine's singing career.

Whatever happens in Celine's personal and professional lives, it is assured that she will be with us for a long time. "There is no limit for me," she has said, "and there never will be."

Discography

Major album releases

1981   *La Voix du bon Dieu (The Voice of God)*
1981   *Celine chante Noël (Celine Sings Christmas)*
1982   *Tellement j'ai d'amour (I Have So Much Love)*
1983   *Chants et contes de Noël (Christmas Songs and Tales)*
1983   *Les Chemins de ma maison (Paths of My House)*
1983   *Du Soleil au coeur (Sunshine in My Heart)*
1984   *Les Plus Grands Succès de Celine Dion* (Compilation) *(Best of Celine Dion)*
1984   *Melanie*
1984   *Les Oiseaux du bonheur* (released only in Europe) *(Birds of Happiness)*
1985   *Celine Dion en concert (Celine Dion in Concert)*
1985   *C'est pour toi (It's for You)*
1986   *Les Chansons en or* (Compilation) *(Golden Songs)*
1987   *Incognito*
1989   *Vivre/The Best of Celine Dion* (released only in Europe) *(Live/The Best of Celine Dion)*
1990   *Unison*

1991 *Dion chante Plamondon (Dion Sings Plamondon)*

1992 *Celine Dion*

1993 *The Color of My Love*

1993 *Les Premières Annees* (Compilation) *(First Years)*

1994 *Celine Dion à l'Olympia (Celine Dion at the Olympia)*

1995 *D'eux* (titled *The French Album* in the USA) *(From Them)*

1996 *Falling into You*

1996 *Gold Volume One*

1996 *Gold Volume Two*

1996 *Celine Dion: In Conversation*

1996 *Live à Paris (Live in Paris)*

1997 *Celine Dion—The Collection 1982–1988*

1997 *C'est Pour Vivre* (Compilation) *(It's for Life)*

1997 *Let's Talk About Love*

Singles

1981 "Ce n'était qu'un rêve" ("It Was Only a Dream")

1982 "Tellement j'ai d'amour pour toi" ("I Have So Much Love for You")

1983 "Mon ami m'a quittée" ("My Friend Left Me")

1983 "D'amour ou d'amitié" ("Love or Friendship")

1984 "Un colombe" ("A Dove")

1985 "C'est pour vivre" ("For Life")

1985 "Fais ce que tu voudras" ("Do What You Want")

1987 "Incognito"

1987 "Lolita (trop jeune pour aimer)" ("Lolita [Too Young to Love]")

1987 "On traverse un miroir" ("We're Crossing a Mirror")

1987 "Délivre-moi" ("Set Me Free")

1988 "Jours de fièvre" ("Feverish Days")

1988 "Comme un coeur froid" ("Like a Cold Heart")

1988 "D'abord c'est quoi l'amour?" ("First of All, What Is Love?")

1990 "The Last to Know"

1990 "(If There Was) Any Other Way"

1990 "Unison"

1991 "Where Does My Heart Beat Now?"

1991 "Last to Know"

1991 "Ziggy"

1991 "Je danse dans ma tête" ("I Dance in My Head")

1991 "L'amour existe encore" ("Love Still Exists")

1991 "Have a Heart"

1992 "If You Asked Me To"

1992 "Des mots qui sonnent" ("The Sound of Words")

1992 "Nothing's Broken but My Heart"

1992 "Beauty and the Beast"

1993 "Love Can Move Mountains"

1993 "Water from the Moon"

1993 "Did You Give Enough Love?"

1994 "Calling You"

1994 "The Power of Love"

1994 "Think Twice"

1995 "Tu m'aimes encore" ("If You Still Love Me")

1995 "To Love You More"

1996 "Because You Loved Me"

1996   "It's All Coming Back to Me Now"
1997   "All by Myself"
1997   "Je sais pas" ("I Don't Know")
1997   "Tell Him"
1998   "Immortality"
1998   "My Heart Will Go On"

On sale November 1998

ON HER WAY

The Shania Twain Story

by Scott Gray

Shania Twain is the reigning goddess of new country music with a truckload of number one hits, album sales to rival those of fellow Canadian divas Celine Dion and Alanis Morissette, scores of major awards (including a Grammy for Best Country Album), and legions of loyal fans around the world. But it took true grit for this sultry songbird to rise from a hardscrabble childhood to megastardom.

After growing up in poverty in the north woods of Canada, singing in bars since the age of eight, and taking care of her younger siblings when their parents died tragically, she was signed to a recording contract. She went on to meet her Prince Charming, superproducer "Mutt" Lange, and together they created the biggest-selling album by a female artist in country-music history. ON HER WAY is the dazzling chronicle of a dynamic, determined woman.

Published by Ballantine Books.
Available in bookstores everywhere.

The dazzling rise of a young country star . . .

DREAM COME TRUE
The LeAnn Rimes Story

by Jo Sgammato

LeAnn Rimes, owner of a huge, God-given voice, was born knowing what she wanted to do and sang with assurance when she was just a toddler. She burst onto the country-music scene with one great song, "Blue," an old-fashioned ballad originally written for the legendary Patsy Cline. Her album of the same name hit the charts at number one, and LeAnn became one of the biggest entertainment stories of the year.

But as young as she was, this overnight sensation was years in the making. Here is the heartwarming story of LeAnn Rimes and her parents, Belinda and Wilbur Rimes, an American family who made a DREAM COME TRUE.

Published by Ballantine Books.
Available wherever books are sold.

HEART SONG
The Story of Jewel

by Scott Gray

Since the release of her debut CD, *Pieces of You*, soulful singer/songwriter Jewel Kilcher has blossomed into, perhaps, the most popular woman in today's music scene. Jewel has touched the world with raw honesty and a voice as beautifully expansive as her native Alaska landscape.

Here are the intriguing details and little-known facts of her life. From a childhood spent on a rustic homestead and her struggle to overcome dyslexia, through weekly gigs at a San Diego coffeehouse and her breakthrough to superstardom, HEART SONG journeys to the core of this original and insightful poet/musician.

Published by Ballantine Books.
Available wherever books are sold.